Leckie
the education publisher
for Scotland

D1581853

Higher
MODERN
STUDIES

For SQA 2019 and beyond

Revision + Practice
2 Books in 1

ISBN 9780008365325

Published by
Leckie & Leckie Ltd
An imprint of HarperCollins Publishers
Westerhill Road, Bishopbriggs, Glasgow, G64 2QT
T: 0844 576 8126   F: 0844 576 8131
leckiescotland@harpercollins.co.uk
www.leckiescotland.co.uk

Publisher: Sarah Mitchell
Project managers: Lauren Murray

Special thanks to
Louise Robb (proofread)
Jouve (layout and illustration)

Printed and bound by CPI Group (UK) Ltd, Croydon CR0 4YY

A CIP Catalogue record for this book is available from the British Library.

Acknowledgements

Images

P25a © chrisdorney / Shutterstock.com; P30a © Atlaspix / Shutterstock.com; P30b © Michael Tubi / Shutterstock.com; P30c © UniversalImagesGroup / Contributor; P30d © Oli Scarff / Staff / Getty Images; P30e © Cornfield / Shutterstock.com; P31 © WPA Pool / Pool / Getty Images; P33 © 360B / Shutterstock.com; P34 © Matt Dunham / AP / Shutterstock; P37 © Jeff Morgan 08 / Alamy Stock Photo; P40 © The Press Association; P42 © Alisdair Macdonald/Shutterstock; P43 © Chris Watt / Stringer / Getty Images; P44 © Jeff J Mitchell / Staff / Getty Images; P47 © Matt Dunham / AP / Shutterstock; P50 © Jeff J Mitchell / Staff / Getty Images; P51 © Ken Jack / Contributor / Getty Images; P52 © Terry Murden / Shutterstock.com; P54 © Stewart Attwood / EPA-EFE / Shutterstock;

P68 © Commons Briefing Papers 79; P71 © Matt Cardy / Stringer / Getty Images; P76 © PAUL ELLIS / Staff / Getty Images; P78 © News UK; P81 © SOPA Images / Contributor / Getty Images; P83 © Telegraph Media Group Limited (2017 and 2019) ; P84 © Lord Ashcroft Polls, https://lordashcroftpolls.com/2019/12/how-britain-voted-and-why-my-2019-general-election-post-vote-poll/; P92 © Jeff J Mitchell / Staff / Getty Images; P94 © The Guardian, May 2019; P95 © Iscotlanda Photography / Shutterstock.com; P97 © SergeBertasiusPhotography / Shutterstock.com; P105 © OLI SCARFF / Stringer / Getty Images; P106 © Gianpaolo Magni/EPA-EFE/Shutterstock; P107 © Oli Scarff / Staff / Getty Images; P111a Taken by Mnbf9rca on English Wikipedia and licensed under the Creative Commons Attribution-Share Alike 2.5 Generic license; P115 © chrisdorney / Shutterstock.com; P117 © Alex Segre / Contributor; P122 © Mary Evans Picture Library / Alamy Stock Photo; P124 © Geoffrey Robinson / Alamy Stock Photo; P126 © Andrew McCaren/LNP/Shutterstock; P128 © Willy Barton / Shutterstock.com; P129 © Iain McGillivray / Shutterstock.com; P131 © WENN Ltd / Alamy Stock Photo; P132 © Steven May / Alamy Stock Photo; P133 © Elena Rostunova / Shutterstock.com; P135 © COSLA / Scottish Government; P136 © Stephen Barnes/Law and Order / Alamy Stock Photo; P 143 © Steve Heap / Shutterstock.com; P144 © lev radin / Shutterstock.com; P146 © Rob Crandall / Shutterstock.com; P148 © YES Market Media / Shutterstock.com; P151 © FREDERIC J. BROWN / Staff / Getty Images; P153 © Bureau of Labour Statistics via Haver Analytical; P156 © Shutterstock.com; P157 © Joe Raedle / Staff / Getty Images; P160 © Center on budget and Policy Priorities.This material was created by the Center on Budget and Policy Priorities (www.cbpp.org); P162 © Jonathan Weiss / Shutterstock.com; P163 © weerapong pumpradit / Shutterstock.com; P167 © Bogdan Cristel/EPA-EFE/Shutterstock.com; P169 © PIUS UTOMI EKPEI / Stringer / Getty Images; P70 © lonndubh / Shutterstock.com; P171 © conejota / Shutterstock.com; P173 © MAHMUD HAMS / Staff / Getty Images; P175 © Anadolu Agency / Contributor / Getty Images; P176 © Hindustan Times / Contributor / Getty Images; P179 © Twocoms/ Shutterstock.com; P184 © Anadolu Agency / Contributor / Getty Images; P185 © MICHAEL URBAN / Staff / Getty Images P207 © YouGov.co.uk; P208a © The Conservative Party; P208b © YouGov.co.uk; P208b © YouGov.co.uk; P209: © Telegraph Media Group Limited (2019); P217b © YouGov.co.uk; P217c © YouGov.co.uk; P221 © http://www.sccjr.ac.uk/wp-content/uploads/2015/10/SCCJR-Whos-in-prison.pdf; P222 © STV News; P223 © Howard League for Penal Reform

All other images from Shutterstock.com

Whilst every effort has been made to trace the copyright holders, in cases where this has been unsuccessful, or if any have inadvertently been overlooked, the Publishers would gladly receive any information enabling them to rectify any error or omission at the first opportunity.

To access the ebook version of this Revision Guide visit
www.collins.co.uk/ebooks
and follow the step-by-step instructions.

INTRODUCTION

The course and the assessment

Part 1: REVISION GUIDE

Democracy in Scotland and the United Kingdom

Contents

Social issues in the United Kingdom: social inequality in the United Kingdom

Social issues in the United Kingdom: crime and the law in the United Kingdom

International issues: world powers – USA

International issues: world issues – terrorism

Part 2: PRACTICE PAPERS

ANSWERS Check your answers to the practice test papers online:

www.collins.co.uk/pages/Scottish-curriculum-free-resources

The course

Complete Revision and Practice

This two-in-one Complete Revision and Practice book is designed to support you as students of Higher Modern Studies. It can be used either in the classroom, for regular study and homework, or for exam revision. By combining a revision guide and two full sets of practice exam papers, this book includes everything you need to be fully familiar with the Higher Modern Studies course and exam.

About the revision guide

The revision guide concisely covers the Higher Modern Studies course content for selected areas of the course to help you prepare for both question papers in the final exam. There are 'Top Tips' throughout the revision guide that emphasise important points and helpful hints. There are also 'Quick Test' questions at the end of each section that will allow you to test your knowledge of the subject matter. SQA sample answers, for Question Paper 2, can also be found within the introductory chapters that will help you work through each type of skills question you will be asked to complete in the exam.

How to use the practice exam papers

This book contains two practice exam papers that replicate the layout, structure and question style of the Higher Modern Studies exam. There are also tips on important exam techniques that will help you gain valuable marks and avoid common mistakes. Marking instructions for each of the exam papers can be accessed online at www.collins.co.uk/pages/Scottish-curriculum-free-resources. Completing a range of unseen exam style questions is an effective study technique to prepare you for the final exam.

The Higher Modern Studies course

The final course award you receive will be based on the marks you achieve in two assessed components:

1. Question papers

The question papers are worth a total of 80 marks:

- Question Paper 1: This essay-based paper is worth a total mark allocation of 52 marks, which represents 47% of the course assessment. In this paper you answer three questions that assess your knowledge and understanding of the course content: two questions are worth 20 marks and one question is worth 12 marks.
- Question Paper 2: This skills-based paper is worth a total mark allocation of 28 marks, which represents 26% of the course assessment. In this paper you answer three questions that assess your ability to: detect and explain the degree of objectivity, draw and support conclusions and evaluate the reliability of a range of sources.

2. The assignment
* The assignment has a total mark allocation of 30 marks. This is 27% of the overall marks for the course assessment.

Rationale

Studying Modern Studies at Higher will build on the knowledge and skills that you developed within Modern Studies at National 5 or across other areas of the curriculum. The course aims to encourage you to think critically about the society we live in, widening your knowledge of political, social and international issues, while encouraging you to consider the values and beliefs of others. As a result, the course will prepare you for your place in society as a responsible citizen who is able to make an effective contribution both at home and beyond.

You will engage in investigative and critical thinking activities, allowing you to work collaboratively with peers as well as developing your skills as an independent learner. Furthermore, you will build on your capacity to evaluate and analyse a wide range of sources, allowing you to make informed decisions, come to valid conclusions, and hone your ability to identify where sources have been selective in the use of facts. These transferable skills will support you as you move on to Further or Higher Education or the world of work.

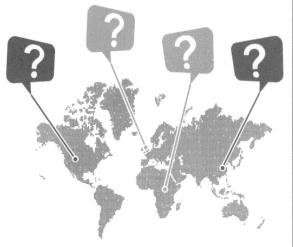

Think about your place in the world

Course outline

The Higher course consists of three units. Within these course units there is considerable choice with regard to the topics studied. This Success Guide offers support for the units shown in the table below.

Unit title	Topics covered in the Success Guide
Political issues	Democracy in Scotland and the United Kingdom
Social issues	• Social inequality in the United Kingdom • Crime and the law in the United Kingdom
International issues	• World powers – the USA • World issues – terrorism

Assessment

The assignment

The assignment is the added value (AVU) element of the course. You may remember this from National 5 Modern Studies or another area of the curriculum. The assignment has two main elements:

1. Research

2. Production of evidence

TOP TIP

Choose an issue that has clear arguments to support or oppose it.

You will choose an area of study that allows you to analyse a complex contemporary issue and apply decision-making skills. You will research the issue, analysing and evaluating sources of evidence. Your teacher can advise during the research element of your assignment but cannot go beyond 'reasonable assistance'. According to the SQA, 'the term "reasonable assistance" is used to balance the need for support with the need to avoid giving too much assistance. Reasonable assistance may be given on a generic basis to a class or group of candidates; for example, advice on how to develop a project plan. It may also be given to candidates on an individual basis. When reasonable assistance is given on a one-to-one basis in the context of something that a candidate has already produced or demonstrated, there is a danger that it becomes support for assessment, and teachers and lecturers need to be aware that this may be going beyond reasonable assistance.'

The assignment is worth 30 marks and is part of the course assessment. The production of evidence element of the assignment takes place under controlled conditions and must be done in a single sitting. You have 1 hour and 30 minutes to complete this using only your Modern Studies research sheet, which consists of two sides of A4.

Course assessment – the exam

The exam will consist of two question papers. It will assess your skills and breadth of knowledge and understanding across the three units of the course.

The first question paper is the essay-based paper and will be divided into three sections in line with the three units covered – (i) Democracy in Scotland and the UK, (ii) Social Issues in the UK and (iii) International Issues. During the course of this paper you will answer three questions: two 20-mark questions and one 12-mark question. There is an element of choice within each of the three sections. The time allocation for Question Paper 1 is 1 hour and 45 minutes.

There are four types of KU question in the final exam, worth between 12 and 20 marks. They involve four key command words/phrases, which are allocated a specific number of marks. These questions can appear in any section of the paper.

Key command word/phrase	Number of marks
Analyse	12
Evaluate	12
To what extent	20
Discuss	20

The front page of Question Paper 1 will look similar to that shown below:

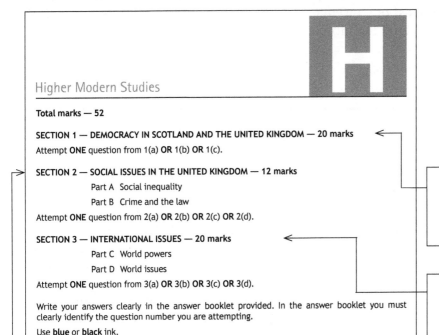

Higher Modern Studies

Total marks — 52

SECTION 1 — DEMOCRACY IN SCOTLAND AND THE UNITED KINGDOM — 20 marks
Attempt **ONE** question from 1(a) **OR** 1(b) **OR** 1(c).

SECTION 2 — SOCIAL ISSUES IN THE UNITED KINGDOM — 12 marks

Part A   Social inequality

Part B   Crime and the law

Attempt **ONE** question from 2(a) **OR** 2(b) **OR** 2(c) **OR** 2(d).

SECTION 3 — INTERNATIONAL ISSUES — 20 marks

Part C   World powers

Part D   World issues

Attempt **ONE** question from 3(a) **OR** 3(b) **OR** 3(c) **OR** 3(d).

Write your answers clearly in the answer booklet provided. In the answer booklet you must clearly identify the question number you are attempting.

Use **blue** or **black** ink.

Before leaving the examination room you must give your answer booklet to the Invigilator; if you do not, you may lose all the marks for this paper.

SECTION 1: Everyone will study Section 1. You will have a choice of three questions.

SECTION 3: In Section 3 you either study 'World Powers' or 'World Issues'. Make sure you pick the correct part to answer. You will have a choice of two questions.

SECTION 2: In Section 2 you either study 'Social Inequality' or 'Crime and the Law'. Make sure you pick the correct part to answer. You will have a choice of two questions.

TOP TIP

Ensure that you are fully aware of which part within each section you should answer questions on. For example, in this paper everyone will answer one knowledge question from Section 1 – **either** 1(a), 1(b) or 1(c). However, you must select the core Part A **or** Part B in Section 2 and between Part C **or** Part D in Section 3.

What is required for 12 and 20 marks?

12-mark questions

In the 12-mark questions, you can be awarded up to a maximum of 8 marks for showing your knowledge and understanding (KU) of the issue. Try to remember to use the SEE system – make a **s**tatement, give an **e**xplanation of that point and support it with relevant **e**xemplification. The remaining 4 marks are awarded for analysis **or** evaluation of the issue.

So for 12 marks you could achieve 8 by demonstrating **at least two** relevant aspects of knowledge, fully explained, which relate closely to the key aspects of the question **supported by** extended, relevant, accurate and up-to-date examples. You could gain the other 4 marks by giving **at least one** insightful, extended, accurate and justified analytical or evaluative comment, which relates closely to the key aspects of the question and is supported by evidence.

- Knowledge – 8
- Analysis/Evaluation – 4

20-mark questions

- For 20 marks, just as for 12-mark questions, you again will be awarded up to a maximum of 8 marks for KU. The remaining marks are awarded for analysis, evaluation/conclusions **and** structure. You could gain up to 6 marks for demonstrating **at least two** developed, relevant and accurate analytical comments that are justified **and** exemplified. These should relate closely to the question and may be linked. A further 4 marks can be awarded for balanced, insightful conclusions that are justified and directly address the central aspects of the question, considering a range of viewpoints. The final 2 marks are awarded for a structure that identifies the issue and presents a clear and consistent line of argument.
- Knowledge – 8
- Analysis – 6
- Conclusion(s)/Evaluative comments – 4
- Structure – 2

If you make more analytical/evaluative points than are required to gain the maximum allocation of marks, these can be credited as knowledge and understanding marks.

'Analyse' questions

You will be asked to identify parts of an issue, the relationship between these parts and their relationships with the whole. You may also be able to draw out and relate implications to certain issues.

For all of the below sample questions with possible responses, all text in blue is a relevant point with an analytical comment and all text in red is a further relevant point giving extended analytical comment. Where green text has been used, this is providing an evaluation/conclusion comment.

Analyse the inequalities faced by certain groups in society.	**12 marks**

Women suffer income inequality. This is evidenced by the Gender Pay Gap. The BBC reported recently that women on average earn 9.4% less than men. This is often attributed to the fact that women take career breaks to have a family and lose valuable experience in the workplace. However, the BBC report also highlighted that the gender pay gap had fallen, with women in the age range of 22–40 earning more than men for the first time. It is further argued that new regulations regarding shared maternity leave should help to bridge the gap in earnings.

The above answer would be worthy of 3/4 marks given that the candidate has made two relevant points with extended analytical comment.

Here are some further 'analyse' questions to consider:
- Analyse the factors that influence voting behaviour.
- Analyse the reasons why health inequalities exist.
- Analyse the impact of crime on offenders.
- Analyse the international influence of the world power you have studied.

'Evaluate' questions

You will be asked to make a judgement based on criteria; to determine the value of something.

Evaluate the effectiveness of prison in tackling crime.	**12 marks**

Prison is effective in that it removes the offender from environments where they have offended, giving them the opportunity to reflect on their actions, potentially access education or treatment programmes, in turn offering them an opening to change once released. However, prisoners serving short-term sentences may not be able to access such programmes due to lack of opportunities in prison and so they may find themselves in identical situations when released. In Scotland, reoffending rates vary; however, in some areas such as Dundee, which has the highest imprisonment rate in Scotland, more than one in three criminals sentenced in the city pick up another conviction within 12 months. This would suggest that short-term prison sentences may have a limited impact on tackling crime.

This would be worthy of 3/4 marks given that the candidate has made two relevant points with extended analytical/evaluative comment.

Here are some further 'evaluate' questions to consider:

- Evaluate the implications of the UK's decision to leave the European Union(EU).
- Evaluate the effectiveness of parliamentary representatives in holding the government to account.
- Evaluate the effectiveness of non-custodial responses to crime.
- Evaluate the social factors that have caused the world issue you have studied.

'To what extent' questions

You will be asked to analyse the issue in the question and come to a conclusion or conclusions that involve evaluative judgement(s) with regard to how accurate the view is. This should be supported with detailed evidence.

> To what extent are parliamentary representatives effective in holding the government to account?
>
> **20 marks**

Parliamentary representatives (MPs) can hold the government to account by voting in the House of Commons (HOC). The division is when MPs are asked to vote on issues in the HOC by physically walking through the 'aye' or 'no' door. For example, recently in the HOC, MPs voted on a Police Grant Report in England and Wales for 2019/20, with 310 voting yes and 254 voting no. this can be an effective way for parliamentary representatives to hold the government to account, especially if the government's own MPs 'rebel' against their government's own agenda. For example, in January 2019, MPs in the HOC voted down Theresa May's Brexit deal. Many Conservative MPs rebelled against the government, leading to a historic defeat. In total, 432 MPs did not support the Prime Minister's deal, many of them from her own party, which consequently led to a vote of no confidence – the ultimate check MPs have in holding the government to account. However, a representative's ability to hold the government to account is greatly reduced by the existence of the whip system. Whips are MPs or members of the House of Lords, who are appointed by each party in Parliament to help organise their party's contribution to parliamentary business. If an MP does not follow the rules, they may be suspended from their party, but keep their seat, or have their whip revoked. They will have to sit as an independent party until their whip is restored. Additionally, if they are a career MP, after being suspended, their career will likely falter. For example, Andrew Griffiths, a conservative MP, had his whip removed for 13 months because of allegations of him sending sexual text messages. On top of that, Charlie Elphike, also from the Conservative Party, was also suspended from his party after two allegations of sexual misconduct in the office. However, they were both reinstated in time for the Brexit votes in 2019. Therefore, it can be concluded that parliamentary representatives can hold the government to account within the chamber by voting against government policies or laws; however, the effectiveness of this tool is limited by the whip system that controls the actions of the majority of representatives.

This extract would be worthy of 6 marks, the maximum allocation for a single issue. The candidate has made two developed points that have included up-to-date exemplification and a sub-conclusion linking back to the question set.

Here are some further 'to what extent' questions to consider:

- To what extent is the media the most important factor influencing voting behaviour?
- To what extent have the government been successful in tackling inequalities?
- To what extent has the government (of the world power you have studied) effectively responded to socio-economic inequality?

'Discuss' questions

In these questions you will communicate ideas and information on the issue in the statement. You will be credited for analysing and evaluating different views of the statement/viewpoint. You should also make a judgement about the accuracy of the statement.

> The political system provides an effective check on the government.
> Discuss with reference to a world power you have studied.   **20 marks**

World power – USA

Within the USA, Congress acts as an effective check on the government in line with constitutional arrangements. However, the President and in turn the government has significant powers that are often difficult for Congress to restrict. The President has the power to veto any bill that Congress has passed, simply returning it unsigned with recommendations as to how it could be amended or improved. President Trump has issued 6 veto's so far (February 2020), whereas President Obama used it on 12 occasions during his two terms in office. However, Congress is able to override any veto of a bill imposed by the President. In order for the veto to be overridden, Congress needs a two-thirds majority in both the Senate and the House of Representatives to vote against it. This appears to be a challenge to Congress as a large number of attempts to override a veto fail. However President Obama's veto regarding the 'Justice Against Sponsors of Terrorism Act'(JASTA) was overturned when Congress secured a 2/3rd in September 2016. It is therefore accurate to state that on certain occasions the political system can be a significant check on the government.

This would be worthy of 5/6 marks given that the candidate has made two developed, relevant and accurate analytical comments that are justified and exemplified. They also relate closely to the question and are linked.

Here are some further 'discuss' questions to consider:

- There are many reasons to explain why health inequalities exist. Discuss.
- Citizens can influence government decision making. Discuss.
- Attempts to resolve (the world issue) have failed. Discuss.
- There are many possible alternatives for the governance of Scotland. Discuss.

TOP TIP

Make sure that you are familiar with the Course Specification, especially pages 4 and 5! Each of the bullet point lists for each section outline what questions can be asked in the final exam! https://www.sqa.org.uk/sqa/47924.html.

Drawing and supporting conclusions

You should be able to draw and support complex conclusions using a range of sources of information. This question is worth 10 marks in the final exam.

The question will have between two and four sources. Sources can be written, numerical, graphical or pictorial. You must make three conclusions and an overall conclusion, using each of the sources at least once across your answer.

Steps to success

1. Make your conclusion using the bullet point as a prompt. Remember that a conclusion is a judgement. You are not awarded any marks for your conclusion; your marks are allocated for your use of supporting evidence.

2. Identify which sources link to each of the bullet points, highlighting the key information from the sources that you will be able to use to support your conclusion.

3. Remember to use ALL the sources – a maximum of 6 marks will be awarded in the exam if all the sources are not used.

4. Write your answer – give your conclusion, followed by your evidence. Three marks are awarded for your use of evidence to support each conclusion. You should aim to link evidence either within or between sources. This is referred to as a synthesis of evidence.

5. The final two marks are awarded for an overall conclusion. Look carefully for any words in bold to help you come to your overall conclusion. For example, look out for words like `**extent**' or `**most**'.

6. You should try to make `**evaluative comments**' within your answer. These are normally comments about numerical evidence, e.g. significant decrease/increase; improved/ deteriorated or majority/minority.

TOP TIP

Use different coloured highlighters to help you write your conclusions. Highlight each bullet point a different colour and highlight the information in the sources that matches with each bullet point the same colour. This will help when structuring your answer.

Sample question

Study Sources A, B and C then attempt the question that follows.

Source A

Minimum unit pricing for alcohol — one year on

On the 1st of May 2018 Scotland became the first country in the world to implement a minimum unit price for alcohol (MUP). The minimum price for alcohol set a floor price for a unit of alcohol at 50p. Drinks like strong white cider, super strength lager and own brand vodka were most affected. It was once possible to buy a 3 litre bottle of strong cider with 22 units of alcohol in it for £3·99 but the same cider now costs £11. The legislation includes a 'sunset clause', meaning that it will expire after six years unless the Scottish Parliament passes an order to extend it. Other UK countries have yet to introduce MUP but are looking to introduce it in the near future.

Analysis of current consumption patterns shows that, within the Scottish population, 14·9% do not drink, 60·5% are moderate drinkers, 19·1% are hazardous drinkers and 5·5% are harmful drinkers. Men still drink more alcohol than women whereas women tend to drink more expensive alcoholic beverages such as wines and gin that MUP doesn't affect. On average, drinkers who live in poverty used to purchase approximately 500 units of alcohol per year, for less than 50p per unit, however after a year of MUP this figure has decreased. Interestingly, this has not been the case with those in better off socio-economic groups (A and B). A critic of MUP argued, 'it is not the prosecco drinking well-to-do in society that minimum pricing affects, it is the everyday person trying to buy a drink that he or she can afford.'

A main aim of MUP is to tackle the social issues associated with alcohol. 60% of young offenders were drunk at the time of their offence, often having consumed strong tonic wine which is priced above 50p per unit. High tariff crimes such as murder and violence show a small decrease in recent years but it is debatable whether this has any relation to MUP. Unexpectedly, MUP may actually be causing a rise in crime as supermarkets have reported an increase in the theft of strong alcohol. With regard to alcohol-related ill health, MUP aims to make dangerous 'binge drinking' more expensive. As 'binge drinking' is a major cause of hospitalisation, it is hoped that alcohol-related ill health will be reduced. Medical experts warn that one 'binge drinking' session is more damaging to the liver than drinking moderately numerous times during the week. The idea that MUP would be the next 'smoking ban' in terms of major health benefits has yet to materialise but signs are looking positive for the future.

Public survey: What effect has MUP had on your alcohol consumption level?

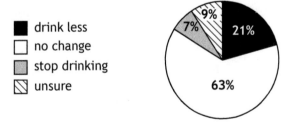

■ drink less
□ no change
▨ stop drinking
▧ unsure

Source B

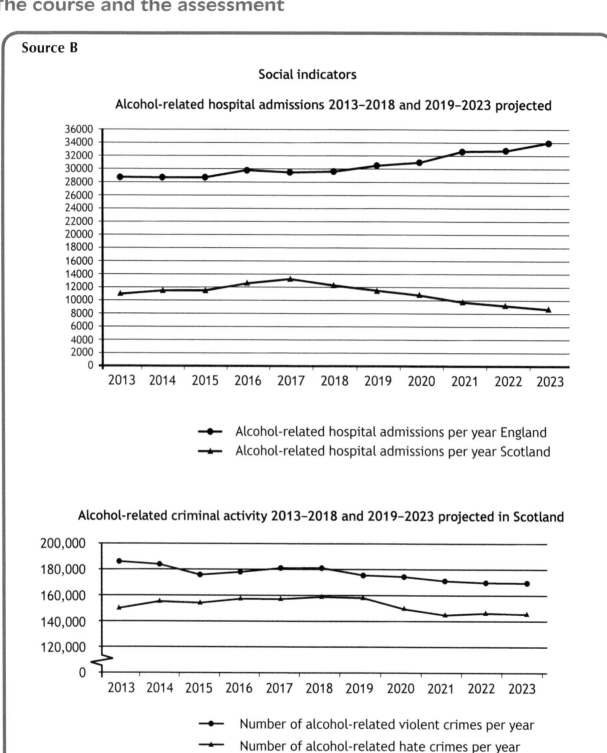

Social indicators

Alcohol-related hospital admissions 2013–2018 and 2019–2023 projected

→●— Alcohol-related hospital admissions per year England
→▲— Alcohol-related hospital admissions per year Scotland

Alcohol-related criminal activity 2013–2018 and 2019–2023 projected in Scotland

→●— Number of alcohol-related violent crimes per year
→▲— Number of alcohol-related hate crimes per year

Source C

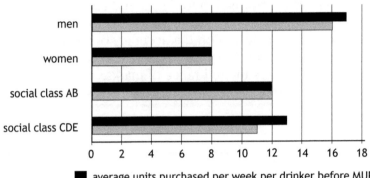

Selected statistics on alcohol consumption rates

Consumption by gender and social class

- ■ average units purchased per week per drinker before MUP
- ▨ average units purchased per week per drinker after MUP

Attempt the following question, using **only** the information in Sources A, B and C above.

What conclusions can be drawn about minimum unit pricing for alcohol in Scotland?

You must draw conclusions about

- minimum unit pricing and consumption by socio-economic group
- minimum unit pricing and crime rates
- minimum unit pricing and health.

You must also make an overall conclusion on the **extent** to which peoples' drinking habits have changed due to minimum unit pricing.

Sample answer

Bullet point 1:

The impact of MUP has lowered consumption levels for poorer people but made no difference to the middle and upper classes. Source C shows that those from social classes CDE drink 2 units less than they did before MUP was introduced, whereas those from social classes AB remain unchanged, still drinking 12 units per week. This is supported by Source A where it states that 'drinkers who live in poverty used to purchase approximately 500 units of alcohol per year, for less than 50p per unit, however after a year of MUP this figure has decreased. Interestingly, this has not been the case with those in better off socio-economic groups (A and B).'

Total — 3 marks (conclusion with synthesis of evidence from Source C and then synthesised with Source A).

Overall conclusion:

I conclude overall that MUP has changed the drinking habits of some groups but the majority of people (63%) have continued to drink in the same way. It has reduced consumption of alcohol in lower class groups but critics argue that it is not the 'prosecco drinking well-to-do in society that minimum pricing affects, it is the everyday person trying to buy a drink that he or she can afford' (Source A). This means it has not worked fully to change drinking habits.

Total — 2 marks (overall conclusion supported by detailed evidence).

Detecting and explaining the degree of objectivity

You should be able to use a range of sources of information to detect and explain how accurate a statement is. In the final exam, this question is worth 10 marks. You must use all the sources provided and make an overall conclusion on the accuracy of the statement to gain full marks. It is important to note that you must provide evidence to support and oppose the statement, otherwise you cannot access the full range of marks.

Steps to success

1. Read the given viewpoint carefully and find key words – you will use these to identify how accurate the statement is.

2. Identify which sources or parts of sources **SUPPORT** the viewpoint – highlight them one colour.

3. Identify which sources or parts of sources **OPPOSE** the viewpoint – highlight them another colour. Remember, you must use **ALL** the sources in your answer at least once.

4. Write your answer. Start by providing evidence to **SUPPORT** the viewpoint in one paragraph, followed by evidence to **OPPOSE** in another paragraph. Collectively, this part of your answer is worth 8 marks. You might find you have more evidence to support than to oppose or vice versa. This is not a problem as it will help you reach your overall conclusion.

5. You should aim to link evidence either within or between sources. This is referred to as a synthesis of evidence.

6. Write you overall conclusion stating **how accurate** the statement is followed by your 'most convincing piece of evidence'. Remember, your overall conclusion can **NEVER** state that the viewpoint is 'totally accurate' or 'totally inaccurate'! This would be wrong and worthy of zero marks.

7. You should try to make '**evaluative comments**' within your answer. These are normally comments about numerical evidence, e.g. significant decrease/increase; improved/ deteriorated or majority/minority.

Sample question

Study Sources A and B then attempt the question that follows.

Source A

Nuclear weapons are the most dangerous weapons in the world. One missile is able to destroy a whole city, kill millions and poison the environment for future generations. Nuclear weapons have only been used twice in warfare, in 1945, however there have been over 2000 nuclear tests since then as countries have competed to increase their military power. The first resolution adopted by the UN General Assembly was to establish a Commission that would seek to control atomic energy and make proposals to eliminate atomic and nuclear weapons from national militaries.

There have been numerous treaties signed between countries to prevent the development of nuclear weapons. In 1968, the Non-Proliferation Treaty (NPT) was signed which recognised five countries as legally possessing nuclear weapons, also referred to as nuclear weapon states. These countries are China, France, Russia, the UK and the USA, and they have all since committed to a process of denuclearisation with a goal of removing all nuclear weapons. However, since then other countries have continued to develop a nuclear weapons stockpile.

In 2010 Russia and the USA signed the New Strategic Arms Reduction Treaty (New START) to replace the previous 1991 START treaty. In the New START treaty, the USA and Russia agreed to reduce their number of strategic warheads. This target was to be achieved by February 2018 and the treaty continues in force until 2021.

Further steps to a nuclear-free world were taken in 2017 with the approval of the treaty on the Prohibition of Nuclear Weapons by 122 countries. Those who have signed the treaty agree to pursue measures on disarmament and to make commitments against the use, development and stockpiling of nuclear weapons. The treaty was signed by the UN Secretary General in November 2017 and has been celebrated as a step towards a nuclear-free world. However, many argue that it will have no practical impact and it faces significant criticism from the five nuclear weapons states who have refused to attend the treaty negotiations.

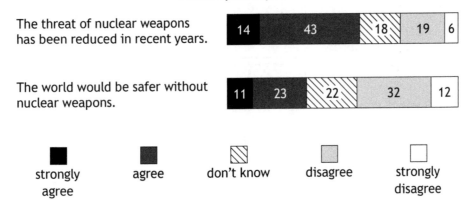

Public opinion poll

The threat of nuclear weapons has been reduced in recent years.
14 | 43 | 18 | 19 | 6

The world would be safer without nuclear weapons.
11 | 23 | 22 | 32 | 12

■ strongly agree   ■ agree   ▨ don't know   ▥ disagree   □ strongly disagree

Source B

Nuclear disarmament — an uncertain future?

Since Donald Trump became President of the United States, tensions and uncertainty in international diplomacy have increased. In Donald Trump's first address to the UN General Assembly he threatened to *'totally destroy'* North Korea if they continue their testing of ballistic missiles. In 2017, North Korea launched 23 missiles in an effort to develop a long-range nuclear warhead. In early 2018, tensions further flared as Donald Trump tweeted that *'I too have a nuclear button, but it is a much bigger and more powerful one than his, and my button works!'* North Korea has now conducted six nuclear tests to prove their ability to fire nuclear weapons.

The process of nuclear disarmament has also faced setbacks in the Middle East where Donald Trump has withdrawn from Barack Obama's 2015 deal with Iran that would have seen UN weapons inspectors enter Iran to ensure that they are not developing nuclear weapons. Many fear that this will lead Iran's President Hassan Rouhani to resume aspects of their nuclear programme. Despite both the USA and Russia meeting their New START targets, the treaty remains controversial. Trump has called the New START treaty a *'bad deal'* which is *'one-sided.'* The treaty will expire in 2021 and so far there has been no initial discussion between the USA and Russia on what could replace it. Whilst some commentators are fearful that Trump will refuse to sign a new deal, others suggest that this is only *'bluster'* and that the advantages and successes of the New START deal so far will improve the likelihood of a renewal of the treaty.

Global nuclear warheads stockpile

Country	1965	1985	2017
Russia	6144	38582	4500
USA	31139	23368	4000
France	32	360	300
China	5	222	270
UK	271	350	214
Pakistan			140
India			130
Israel		42	80
North Korea			15
Total	37591	62924	9649

Attempt the following question, using **only** the information in Sources A and B above.

To what extent is it accurate to state that efforts to reduce the threat posed by nuclear weapons have been successful?

Sample answer

Evidence supporting the viewpoint:

The statement is supported by evidence because there has been a reduction in the number of nuclear weapons. Source A shows that in 2010 the New START Treaty between the US and Russia set a target of reducing their strategic warheads by February 2018. Source B shows that both Russia and America achieved this target, Russia with a massive reduction of over 30,000 since 1985. Source B also shows that the 'advantages and successes of the New START deal so far will improve the likelihood of a renewal of the Treaty' in 2021, showing that the process of nuclear disarmament should continue.

Total — 3 marks (synthesis of evidence from Sources A and B with evaluative comment).

Overall conclusion:

Overall it is only true to a very small extent to say that the efforts to reduce the threat have been successful because the President of the USA has clearly been threatening other countries with use of nuclear weapons and so whilst they have fewer warheads than in the past, the threat remains a significant one as only one missile could create significant destruction. (2 marks)

Evaluating the reliability of sources

You should be able to assess the reliability of sources of information. This question is worth 8 marks in the final exam.

The question will have three sources. The sources can be written, numerical, graphical or pictorial. You must comment on the reliability of each sources before making a conclusion about which source is the most reliable.

Steps to success

1. Take each source in turn and study them carefully. Commenting on each source is worth 2 marks so you should aim to identify two issues that make the source either reliable or unreliable.

2. When writing your answer, you should start with phrases such as *'the source is mostly reliable and trustworthy'*; *'the source is not reliable'*; *'the source is reliable to a certain extent'* and *'the source is trustworthy'*.

3. As you comment on the reliability of the sources, you might wish to consider issues such as: **contents**, **date**, **author**, **adaptation**, **source**, **omission** and **scale**.

4. The final two marks are awarded for making a conclusion about which of the three sources is most reliable. You should pick <u>only one source</u> and compare it to the other sources to ensure that you access the full allocation of marks.

Sample question & extract answer

Study Sources A, B and C then attempt the question that follows.

Source A

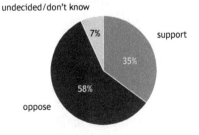

Only a third of Scots support independence

Q. *The second question will ask whether you agree or disagree with a proposal to extend the powers of the Scottish Parliament to enable Scotland to become an independent country, separate from the UK. If the referendum was held tomorrow, would you vote to agree or disagree with this proposal:*

undecided/don't know

7%

support

35%

58%

oppose

Sample size: 1,002 Scottish adults, 18+, 25th–29th August 2011

Source: Ipsos Mori 2011 (international polling company)

Source B

Source: Vote Leave, official campaign in favour of the UK leaving the European Union, 2016

Source C

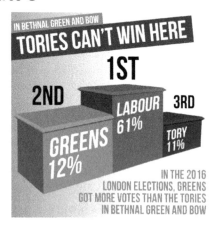

> **TOP TIP**
>
> As you work your way through this question, circle or highlight any issues that you think you can comment on. Remember to look for omission – things that have been left out. Also, look carefully at how sources are presented – is the scale correct or does it skew the way someone might view the source! Look at the 2019 question on this page.

Source: The Green Party, 2017 election leaflet

Attempt the following question, using **only** the information in Sources A, B and C above.

To what extent are Sources A, B and C reliable?

You must provide an overall conclusion on the most reliable source of information.

Sample answer

Evaluating the reliability of source:

Source B can be viewed as not being reliable as it comes from a political campaign group (Vote Leave) and could be biased. It also gives a figure (£350m per week) but hasn't included any evidence or a reference as to where the information came from. This makes it difficult to check this figure and therefore calls into question how reliable this source is.

Total — 2 marks (detailed evidence provided)

Providing an overall conclusion on most reliable source:

Source A is the most reliable source as it comes from a reputable source and contains a very high number of respondents to the survey. The information may be out of date; however, when compared to the other two sources, which come from potentially biased organisations such as political parties and campaign groups, it is the most reliable of the three.

Total — 2 marks (overall conclusion supported by detailed evidence from all sources)

The assignment

In order to complete Higher Modern Studies you must undertake an assignment – you may recall completing something similar in National 5 Modern Studies or other subjects. The assignment will give you the opportunity to show the application of skills as well as knowledge and is worth 30 marks (27% of the total mark). It is therefore of paramount importance that the assignment is completed to a high standard.

Your assignment will be based on a complex contemporary issue that allows for analysis and the application of decision-making skills.

Stages

The assignment has **two** key stages:

1. Research
2. Production of evidence

Research stage

At this initial stage you need to:

- Identify an issue.
- Collect a range of evidence.
- Analyse, evaluate and synthesise information from a range of sources.
- Reach a decision while showing an awareness of alternative viewpoints.

Production of evidence stage

This stage involves writing up your assignment, under exam conditions, in the format of a report. You will be able to take 'specified resources' into the write-up. The SQA refer to this as **research evidence**. This is evidence you will have collected during the research stage. This evidence should consist of no more than two single-sided sheets of A4 and will be submitted to the SQA with your written report. The research evidence may include:

- Evidence/data from primary or secondary research.
- Bullet points/headings/mind maps.
- Statistical, graphical or numerical data.
- Survey results.
- Interview questions and/or answers.
- Questionnaire and/or results.
- List of internet search results.
- Newspaper article or extracts.
- Summary notes taken from a visit or talk/written or audio-visual source.

It is important to remember that your research evidence should be used as a **prompt**. You must **not** simply copy information directly from the research evidence into the assignment.

Planning the assignment

In order to achieve the best possible outcome, a high degree of planning and preparation is required.

Selecting your issue for research

Think of the different topics and issues you have looked at in Modern Studies. Create a mind map of the different topics and issues that you could choose to study.

When considering the topic for research, think about whether a decision on the topic can be made – the most suitable topics are those where there are a number of possible options or alternatives (courses of action).

Selecting your methods of research and gathering evidence

Your methods of research can be both quantitative and qualitative and can comprise both primary and secondary data (see list on previous page). The methods of research and sources of evidence selected will depend on your chosen topic and the access you have to different methods; however, you should aim to have used at least three different methods of research.

Ensure that the information gathered when researching is relevant; note where it originated from on your research evidence sheet. It would be worthwhile selecting five or six sources of information to support you at the production of evidence stage.

It is also worth noting how useful and reliable this information has been as you can gain up to 2 marks for commenting on validity, reliability, bias and the status of the source – official report, statistics, etc.

TOP TIP

Remember when using the internet that it comprises a variety of different sources of information: websites, newspaper articles, government reports, blogs, official statistics. Too often candidates refer to research as simply 'using the internet' and give a generic account of the advantages and disadvantages. Ensure that you give specific information regarding which research sources you have used.

Research evidence example

Below are some examples of research evidence gathered for 'Tackling soaring obesity levels in the UK'. A maximum of two sides of A4 should be taken into the write-up stage of the assignment. This should be used as a prompt when writing the assignment up under exam conditions.

Online research into unhealthy foods

Newspaper research into fat taxes

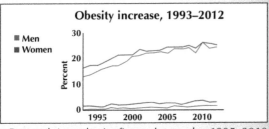

Online research into NHS weight loss surgeries

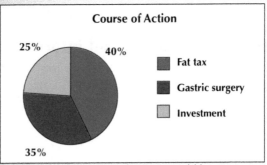

Survey – Which course of action would be most beneficial in tackling soaring levels of obesity in the UK?

Research into obesity figures by gender, 1995–2010

Interview with GP

Writing the report

Given that the assignment is worth 30 marks, it is crucial that you understand where these marks come from. They are broken down as follows:

- Knowledge and understanding of the issue/alternative courses of action – 10 marks
- Use of sources to support your arguments/recommendations (analysis/synthesis) – 10 marks
- Structure (report format) – 4 marks
- Evaluation of sources (validity, reliability, bias) – 2 marks
- Overall decision/conclusion – 4 marks

Possible structure for 'report format' assignment

Title

Begin with the title; you could use your surname, for example, 'The Allardyce Report' and then add the focus, for example 'Tackling soaring obesity levels in the UK'.

Section 1 – role, remit and responsibility

Identify the issue that you have chosen to research. Give an explanation as to why this topic is relevant:

My name is Dianne Allardyce and I am a health policy advisor. I have been tasked by the UK government to undertake significant research with a focus on addressing the soaring levels of obesity in the UK. It is clear that there are three potential courses of action and on conclusion of this research I aim to make a clear recommendation to the UK government on which course of action is most suitable to address this issue.

Section 2 – background information

This should be background information relating to the problem. In this case, statistics to highlight the growth in obesity in adults and children, links to health and wealth inequalities, links to the variety of killer diseases, long-term impact on health, costs to the NHS, etc.

Potential courses of action:

- 'Fat tax' – introduction of a surcharge on fattening foods and drinks.

- 'Investment in education' – increased funding of education programmes in schools to promote healthy living and lifestyles.

- 'Gastric surgery' – resources provided to accommodate further gastric surgery procedures on those regarded as morbidly obese – short-term cost to give a long-term gain.

Sections 3–5

Sections 3–5 will outline the arguments for and against your potential courses of action. You should indicate the impact that each course of action would have on certain areas of society, e.g. government and opposition parties, taxation, social policy, human rights, relationships with other countries, etc.

You must synthesise between sources and where possible use evaluative language (remember to annotate your margin where you have made reference to specific sources of evidence on your research evidence sheet).

Section 3 – 'fat tax'

Outline the arguments to support your recommendation:

3.1

3.2

3.3

Outline the arguments against your recommendation:

3.4

3.5

3.6

Section 4 – 'investment in education'

Outline the arguments to support your recommendation:

4.1

4.2

4.3

Outline the arguments against your recommendation:

4.4

4.5

4.6

Section 5 – 'gastric surgery'

Outline the arguments to support your recommendation:

5.1

5.2

5.3

Outline the arguments against your recommendation:

5.4

5.5

5.6

Section 6 – conclusion

Make a decision – use your knowledge and understanding of the issue and your analysis of it to make a decision about what the best courses of action would be in this situation.

Section 7 – methodologies

Evaluation of the usefulness and reliability of the sources of information you have used on your research evidence sheet.

Higher
MODERN STUDIES

For SQA 2019 and beyond

Revision Guide

Patrick Carson and
Donna Millar

The UK political system

The UK constitutional arrangement

The UK has no formal written constitution; that is, no single document where laws, rules and practices on how the state is governed is set out. As a result, the UK is often referred to as having an 'uncodified' constitution – in that there is no single reference source. However, this is misleading as the governing laws and practices of the UK are written in a variety of documents: statute law (Acts of Parliament), EU law (note: when this book was being revised, the UK was in the process of leaving the EU so this may no longer apply) and ruling judgements from court decisions, and the constitutional arrangement highlights clearly the different branches of government and their respective roles and functions.

The diagram below appears to show that the monarch is the most powerful branch; however, over time the power once held by the monarch has been attributed to parliament. This is often referred to as 'parliamentary sovereignty'. Parliamentary sovereignty ensures that the UK Parliament has overall legal authority, which means it has the power to devise, amend or terminate any law. However, the diagram below also highlights the changes to parliamentary sovereignty in recent years, i.e. the creation of devolved bodies, with the transfer of significant powers to the Scottish Parliament, the Welsh Assembly and the Northern Ireland Assembly. Furthermore, parliamentary sovereignty has been limited as a result of political change both inside and outside the UK.

The Queen – Head of State

Boris Johnson – PM
Head of Government
Executive Branch

MPs/Lords
House of Commons/Lords
Legislative Branch

Supreme Court
Judges
Judicial Branch

Devolved Bodies – MSPs
The Scottish Parliament
(devolved matters)

The UK constitutional arrangement

TOP TIP

Use the following link to identify further evidence of developments that have affected parliamentary sovereignty: https://www.parliament.uk/about/how/role/sovereignty/

got it? ☐ ☐ ☐

The monarch is still regarded as Head of State; however, her role in parliament is clearly viewed as one of carrying out traditional and ceremonial functions, including appointing the Prime Minister, dissolving parliament and delivering the speech marking the beginning of the parliamentary year. However, we must understand fully what each of the other branches does.

State opening of parliament

The branches of the UK constitutional arrangement

Executive branch (Prime Minister and cabinet)

The Prime Minister is head of the UK government. He is ultimately responsible for all policy and decisions. He oversees the operation of the Civil Service and government agencies, appoints members of the government and is the key government figure in the House of Commons.

Legislative branch (House of Commons and House of Lords)

This branch of the constitutional arrangement examines and challenges the work of the government – this is called scrutiny. It debates and discusses government policy, proposed legislation and current issues. It approves and passes all new laws and it therefore enables the government to raise taxes.

Judicial branch (courts)

This branch is responsible for interpreting the law and deciding on legal disputes.

Devolved bodies: Scottish Parliament, Welsh Assembly, Northern Ireland Assembly

Takes responsibility for devolved powers. Devolved powers are decisions that the UK Parliament controlled in the past. This could include matters like education or health.

Quick Test

1. Describe what is meant by the term 'uncodified constitution'.
2. Explain, in detail, the importance of parliamentary sovereignty.
3. Using the website from the Top Tip, list three further laws that affected parliamentary sovereignty.
4. Summarise the roles and functions of each of the branches of government: executive, legislative and judicial.

The role and powers of UK central government

Government and parliament are often confused with one another. They do, however, work closely together as they both play a part in forming the laws of the United Kingdom. However, they are separate institutions with separate functions.

Government	Parliament
The government runs the country. It has responsibility for developing and implementing policy and for drafting laws. It is also known as the 'executive'.	Parliament is the highest legislative authority in the UK. It has responsibility for checking the work of the government and examining, debating and approving new laws. It is also known as the 'legislature'.

Forming a government

The political party that wins an overall majority in the House of Commons after a general election forms the new government and by consequence the party leader becomes the Prime Minister (PM). In 2015, the Conservative Party had the majority of seats with 331 and as a result David Cameron became Prime Minister for a second term. However, when no one single party wins a majority of seats the largest party may form a minority government or there may be a coalition government formed, as was the case in 2010 when the Conservative Party joined with the Liberal Democrats, with David Cameron becoming the Prime Minister and Nick Clegg, the leader of the Liberal Democrats, his Deputy. More recently, when Prime Minister Theresa May called an election in 2017, the Conservatives lost their overall majority in the House of Commons and entered into a 'confidence and supply' agreement with the Democratic Unionist Party (DUP) in which the Conservative government agreed to increase funding for Northern Ireland in exchange for the DUP voting with the Conservatives on certain issues. The Prime Minister then has the task of appointing ministers who work in the government departments; the most senior of these ministers sit in the Cabinet.

The role of the Prime Minister

The Prime Minister is head of the UK government. He or she is ultimately responsible for all policy and decisions, providing political leadership and the political direction to be taken by the government, setting key priorities and strategies. The PM oversees the operation of the Civil Service and government agencies, appoints members of the Cabinet and is the principal government figure in the House of Commons.

Powers of the PM

Patronage

This is the power to appoint someone to an important position. The PM can appoint Cabinet ministers, initiate Cabinet reshuffles, appoint life peers and make recommendations within the honours system. For example, when Boris Johnson became Prime Minister in July 2019, he appointed Sajid Javid as Chancellor.

Authority within the Cabinet system

The PM chairs the Cabinet meetings and manages their agenda; that is, their length and frequency, as well as directing and summing up the Cabinet discussion.

Boris Johnson

Party leadership – the leader of the largest party in the House of Commons

A large working majority can strengthen the power of the PM as the governing party is able to deliver its manifesto and policy commitments with ease. However, both Theresa May and her successor Boris Johnson, having no overall majority in the Commons, had to rely on the support of the DUP during the period of the supply-and-confidence agreement. This gave the DUP significant influence, particularly in relation to the terms of the UK's withdrawal agreement from the European Union.

Public standing – high public profile

The Prime Minister provides political leadership at home and represents the UK on the international stage. He or she has regular discussions with other world leaders and attends formal meetings of heads of state: EU, G20 summits and the UN. Theresa May spoke about the need for international cooperation to tackle climate change and global inequality when she addressed the United Nations General Assembly in September 2018.

Policy-making

The PM's power to influence policy is not limited to one area – the Prime Minister has the ability to get involved across all areas of responsibility, especially areas where there is a particular interest. Theresa May took a keen interest in the promotion of grammar schools and increasing access to them for children of poorer families. She made it a condition that any existing grammar school that wished to apply for extra funding through the £50m 'growth fund' had first to show that they had improved access to children from poorer backgrounds.

Role and powers of government

A Cabinet meeting

Government departments and their agencies are responsible for putting government policy into practice. Some departments, like the Ministry of Defence, cover the whole of the UK. Others don't – the Department of Health doesn't cover Scotland, Wales and Northern Ireland as this matter is devolved to their respective parliament and assemblies.

The government, i.e. the Prime Minister and government ministers, is supported by the Civil Service. The Civil Service is politically neutral and must serve the government of the day, regardless of the party in power. The Civil Service is responsible for the practical and administrative work of the government. PMs will often also use special advisors who are sometimes referred to as 'spin doctors'. They are often viewed as manipulating information in order to preserve the reputation of the PM or the government.

TOP TIP

For further information on the role and powers of UK central government visit gov.uk: www.gov.uk/government/how-government-works

Quick Test

1. Outline the difference between government and parliament.
2. Explain how the government is formed.
3. Why does government not have full responsibility for all policy areas in the UK?

The role and powers of the devolved bodies

The devolution process throughout the late 1990s led to the creation of a separate Parliament in Scotland and a National Assembly in both Wales and Northern Ireland. The process gave the decision making bodies the **power to legislate** on **devolved matters**, often areas where regional differences exist, while Westminster retained control of **reserved matters** – areas that affect the UK as a whole or those with an international element.

Scottish Parliament

The Scottish Parliament building in Edinburgh

The Scotland Act 1998 was the initial Act of the UK Parliament that passed powers to legislate on devolved matters. These powers were extended by the Scotland Act of 2012.

Devolved matters	Reserved matters
✓ Agriculture, forestry and fisheries	✗ Benefits and social security
✓ Education and training	✗ Immigration
✓ Environment	✗ Defence
✓ Health and social services	✗ Foreign policy
✓ Housing	✗ Employment
✓ Law and order (including the licensing of air weapons)	✗ Broadcasting
	✗ Trade and industry
✓ Local government	✗ Nuclear energy, oil, coal, gas and electricity
✓ Sport and the arts	✗ Consumer rights
✓ Tourism and economic development	✗ Data protection
✓ Many aspects of transport	✗ The Constitution

Since 1999, the powers of the Scottish Parliament have been increased by two further Scotland Acts passed in 2012 and 2016, giving the Scottish Parliament power over a wide range of issues including a Scottish rate of income tax, speed limits, drink driving limits, abortion and air passenger duty.

TOP TIP

The Scotland Act lists the matters that are reserved to the UK Parliament in Schedule 5 – if the matter is not listed in this section, it is devolved to the Scottish Parliament.

The Scottish Parliament can, however, ask the UK government to legislate on devolved matters that they may be considering for England – this is known as a Legislative Consent Motion, sometimes referred to as Sewel Motions. In certain circumstances it can be sensible and advantageous for Scotland to be included in a Westminster bill that refers to a devolved matter; for example, in April 2017 the Scottish Parliament agreed to the relevant points of the Criminal Finances Act that related to the recovery of criminal proceeds.

Welsh Assembly and Northern Ireland Assembly

The Northern Ireland Assembly building

Like the Scottish Parliament, the Assemblies have power to legislate on a number of areas. The Welsh Assembly held its first election in 1999, while the Northern Ireland Assembly had held its first election the year before (in June 1998). However, at the time this book was written, as a result of ongoing disagreements between the DUP and Sinn Féin, the Northern Ireland Assembly had been suspended, for three years with power returning to Westminster. It was not until January of 2020 that a deal was struck between the two main parties, Sinn Fein and the DUP, to reestablish the devolved government of Northern Ireland.

Welsh Assembly devolved matters	Northern Ireland Assembly devolved matters
• Agriculture, fisheries, forestry and rural development • Ancient monuments and historic buildings • Culture • Economic development • Education and training • The environment • Fire and rescue services and the promotion of fire safety • Food • Health and health services • Highways and transport • Housing • Local government • Public administration • Social welfare • Sport and recreation • Tourism • Town and country planning • Water and flood defence • The Welsh language	• Health and social services • Education • Employment and skills • Agriculture • Social security • Pensions and child support • Housing • Economic development • Local government • Environmental issues, including planning • Transport • Culture and sport • The Northern Ireland Civil Service • Equal opportunities • Justice and policing

More recently, reforms to the Welsh devolution settlement have seen more powers being allocated to the Welsh Assembly including powers over such things as ports, speed limits, bus and taxi regulation. Greater powers over taxes such as a Land Transaction tax affecting house purchases and some aspects of income tax have also been transferred.

The logo of the Welsh Assembly

Quick Test

1. Outline the difference between a devolved and reserved matter.
2. Which power does the Scottish Parliament have that neither of the Assemblies has?
3. Have a look at the information on this website and outline what the main issues are that divide the two main parties in the Northern Ireland Assembly: https://www.bbc.co.uk/news/uk-northern-ireland-politics-41723268

The arguments for and against Britain's membership of the European Union

Since the Brexit referendum in 2016 there has been a fierce debate in the UK about the advantages and disadvantages of remaining in or leaving the European Union. At the time of writing, the UK had only recently formally withdrawn from the EU and had entered the so called 'transition phase' to reach a future agreement about relations between the UK and the EU. In order to understand the issue, it is necessary to examine some of the main arguments in favour of 'remain' and 'leave'.

What are the main arguments for 'remain'?

The UK in the world: as a member of the EU with a combined population of over 500 million people and 28 countries, the UK has more influence in the world than if it was acting on its own.

The EU building in Brussels

Sovereignty (i.e. control over its own affairs): although the UK has accepted most EU laws, it has 'opted' out of some such as the Shengen Agreement, which did away with border controls between member states. The UK has more opt outs than any other EU member.

Security: threats such as terrorism and international organised crime are more effectively tackled as part of an organisation like the EU.

EU spending in the UK: EU spending in the UK is approximately £4 billion per year.

Trade: as a member of the EU, the UK has access to a huge market for its goods and services, with few restrictions.

Employment: it is estimated that approximately 3 million jobs in the UK rely on trade with the EU. Some sections of the UK economy, such as nursing and hospitality, rely on workers coming from other EU countries.

Prices and choice: UK consumers benefit from a wider variety of products and lower prices on goods from the EU.

What are the main arguments for 'leave'?

The UK in the world: being a member of the EU limits the UK's international influence. For example, the UK does not have an individual place in the World Trade Organisation (WTO).

Sovereignty (i.e. control over its own affairs): the UK would take back control of all law making and would no longer be 'bound' by EU laws.

Security: The UK will have better control over its own security at the borders and will be able to control immigration to suit its own needs.

EU spending in the UK: although the EU spends about £4 billion each year in the UK, Britain contributes £9 billion more than this to the EU budget.

Trade: as a member of the EU, Britain is prevented from doing its own trade deals with major economies such as the USA, Japan, India and the UAE.

Employment: many small and medium-sized businesses complain that EU rules and regulations ('red tape') make it more difficult and expensive to trade with the EU member states.

Jobs: Britain will be able to increase jobs by controlling immigration and doing trade deals with other countries.

Prices and choice: the price of some goods sold in the UK from the EU are increased due to EU VAT and agricultural subsidies.

TOP TIP

Visit the website of Full Fact: https://fullfact.org/europe/uk-jobs-and-eu/ to find out more about the issues involved in the 'Brexit' debate

Quick Test

1. Summarise the two arguments for 'remain' and two for 'leave' that you think are most important.

2. Following Britain's withdrawal from the EU, there will be a transition period. Visit the website of the Institute for Government (https://www.instituteforgovernment.org.uk/explainers/brexit-transition-period) and explain what this means and what will happen during that period.

The Scottish Independence debate

Since the creation of the Scottish Parliament in 1999, the SNP has continually called for a referendum on independence, their flagship policy – allowing the public to vote on whether to remain as part of the UK or move to become a separate country. In 2012, the governments of Scotland and the UK signed the Edinburgh Agreement in which it was agreed to hold a referendum on independence for Scotland:

'to make provision, in accordance with paragraph 5A of Part 1 of Schedule 5 to the Scotland Act 1998, for the holding of a referendum in Scotland on a question about the independence of Scotland.'

Indyref 2 - the debate about a second referendum

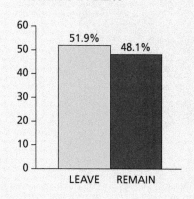

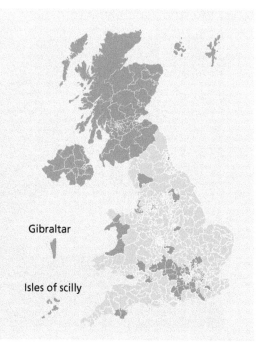

Scotland voted heavily in favour of Remain

In September of 2014, voters in Scotland took part in the referendum to decide 'Should Scotland be an independent country?' The result of that referendum showed a majority of those who voted were against Scottish independence, with 55.3% voting 'No' and 44.7% voting 'Yes'. Following the referendum, the then Prime Minster, David Cameron, declared that 'The debate has been settled for a generation...there can be no disputes, no re-runs. We have heard the settled will of the Scottish people.'

In making this statement, he was reflecting the view of the leader of the SNP, Alex Salmond, who stated on the BBC's Andrew Marr show, prior to the vote, that 'this is a once in a generation, perhaps even a once in a lifetime, opportunity for Scotland.'

Despite the result of the 2014 referendum and the 'once in a generation' statements made by Alex Salmond, his successor as SNP leader and First Minister, Nicola Sturgeon, argued that, as the SNP's policy was to achieve independence within the European Union, then any change to Scotland's position within Europe as a result of being 'forcibly taken out of Europe against its will', would constitute a 'material change of circumstance'. This, she argued, would justify a second independence referendum – Indyref 2.

So, in 2016, when the people of the UK were asked if they wanted to leave or remain in the EU, 51.89% voted Leave and 48.11% voted Remain. This, the SNP claimed, amounted to a 'material change' that would see Scotland taken out of the EU against its will. In Scotland, the overwhelming majority voted to remain in the EU (62% to 38%) in contrast to other parts of the UK, such as England and Wales, where the majority voted 'Leave'. However, because the decision to allow a second referendum lies with the UK government, it is unlikely that a second referendum will be agreed to.

Following his appointment by Prime Minister Boris Johnson in July 2019, the Scottish Secretary, Alister Jack, when asked how he would respond to a request to hold a second referendum, stated that his advice to the Prime Minister would be 'To decline. To refuse it. We settled that in 2014. It's not back on the agenda.'

It is, however, unlikely that the issue of Indyref 2 will be settled in the near future, particularly since the polls have shown increased support for independence following the Brexit referendum and the appointment of Boris Johnson as leader of the Conservative Party and UK Prime Minister.

Quick Test

1. Describe the outcome of the EU referendum across the whole of the UK and how this compared with Scotland.

2. How does Nicola Sturgeon justify a second referendum on Scottish independence?

3. What other factor is said to have increased support in Scotland for a second referendum?

Representative democracy in the UK

Democracy = Rule by the People

The UK is a representative democracy: UK citizens elect representatives to make decisions on their behalf. In the UK, we currently elect a number of representatives, e.g. MPs, MSPs, MEPs and local councillors. These representatives work for us in their respective parliaments and committees and remain in post until the electorate vote them out of office or they resign.

Advantages of representative democracy

- Practical form of participation.
- Ordinary citizens do not have the constant responsibility of decision making.
- Governments should consist of interested, knowledgeable members with relevant experience.

Referenda

UK citizens can, however, still be consulted on major decisions through a referendum (a vote on a single issue); for example, the referendum in 2014 on whether Scotland would become an independent country, or the UK-wide referendum in 2016 on the UK's membership of the European Union.

Democracy in the UK

UK citizens vote every five years to elect MPs who will represent us in the House of Commons, discussing and debating matters and voting on bills that may or may not become law. By electing a Member of Parliament we are giving over our power to a representative, ultimately withdrawing from the decision-making process. If we are content with our MP in the House of Commons, we continue to elect them for a number of years. Following the election in 2019, Conservative MP Peter Bottomley was the longest-serving MP in the Commons, becoming the Father of the House having been an MP since 1975.

Peter Bottomley

Democracy in Scotland

In Scotland, elections to the Scottish Parliament take place every four years – so far in 1999, 2003, 2007, 2011 and 2016 – with 129 MSPs elected to represent the people of Scotland. The five-year gap between the 2011 and 2016 Scottish elections was the result of an agreement between the Scottish and UK governments to avoid the Scottish and UK elections taking place in the same year. It was felt that this might affect voter turnout and might also cause confusion as the Scottish and UK elections use different forms of voting.

The Scottish Parliament

Quick Test

1.   In which way do the majority of citizens participate in a representative democracy?
2.   List the advantages of a representative democracy.
3.   Why was there a five-year gap between the 2011 and 2016 Scottish elections?

Role and influence of MPs

MPs are elected by the UK electorate to represent their interests and concerns in the House of Commons. MPs are involved in considering and proposing new laws, and can use their position to ask government ministers questions about current issues.

MPs divide their time between working in the parliament, in their constituency and for their political party. Constituents can contact their MP in a number of ways to try to gain their support, including visiting their MP's surgery, lobbying them in parliament or by email or telephone.

An MP's constituency office

Influence in parliament

TOP TIP

Remember, MPs in Scotland deal with constituents' problems around **reserved** matters only.

MPs have a number of opportunities to influence decision making in parliament, holding the government to account, while working on behalf of their constituents.

Prime Minister's Question Time

Each Wednesday the PM takes questions in the House of Commons for 30 minutes. This allows backbenchers (MPs who hold no governmental office) to ask questions on behalf of their constituents. In most cases, the session starts with a routine 'open question' from an MP about the Prime Minister's engagements. MPs can then ask supplementary questions on any subject, often one of current political significance. Opposition MPs follow up on this or another topic, usually led by the Leader of the Opposition. Usually, he or she is the only MP allowed to come back with further questions. Examples of typical question topics include equality, parliamentary reform and spending cuts.

Question Time

Question Time in the House of Commons is an opportunity for MPs to question government ministers about matters for which they are responsible. Question Time takes place in the first hour of business each day.

Debating

Frequently, issues concerning the country will be debated at length. MPs can contribute to such debates, particularly if they are of direct concern to their constituents. Issues such as firearms, immigration, terrorism, and the NHS are often debated on the floor of the House of Commons.

Adjournment debates

The half-hour adjournment debate offers another opportunity for MPs to raise matters. Usually taken as the last business of the day, MPs must either win a ballot or be chosen by the Speaker to voice their concern. MPs can also raise matters in debates in Westminster Hall. These are similar to adjournment debates in the Chamber but take place on Tuesdays and Wednesdays and may last for either half an hour or an hour and a half.

Voting

MPs are often required to vote on the passing of legislation or decisions relating to international issues. In May of 2019, MPs voted to make the UK Parliament the first in the world to declare an 'environment and climate emergency'. How your MP votes in Parliament may determine whether you continue to support them or not. This link allows you to find your local MP and see how they voted on key issues: www.theyworkforyou.com

Select Committees

These committees check and report on areas ranging from the work of government departments to economic affairs. The results of these inquiries are public and many require a response from the government. The Home Affairs Committee have recently held high-profile inquiries into the police, the media and criminal investigations.

Private Members' Bills

An MP might introduce a Private Members' Bill in an attempt to pass a new law. Each year, 20 MPs are selected from a ballot and are given the opportunity to bring their own bill forward and have it debated in parliament. Some MPs might use it as an opportunity to highlight a controversial issue, while others might want to make a small change to the law. For example, in 2018, the MP Peter Kyle introduced the Representation of the People (Young People's Enfranchisement) Bill, which sought to reduce the voting age to 16 in parliamentary and other elections. However, few of these bills are successful because of time constraints and the support required from other MPs.

Pressures faced by MPs

When an MP votes or speaks in Parliament they have to consider a number of different pressures and demands on them. Often these pressures will conflict and the MP must make a judgment about which ones are most important in any particular situation. In some cases the MP will simply have to follow the instructions of their local and national party, even when they may hold different views.

Constituents – the people who live in the area represented by the MP will expect their MP to 'fight' for their interests but this may not always be in line with the national party's policies. An example of this was seen in the period before the 2019 election. Some Labour MPs representing constituencies that voted strongly for Brexit did not support their party's policy to hold a second referendum.

Constituency party – each of the main parties has a an organisation in each constituency that selects the candidates, helps at election time, raises funds etc. The choice of MP is not, however, entirely in the hands of the local constituency as the central party will draw up an 'approved' list of candidates to choose from.

Party Whips – each party in Parliament expects its MPs to vote with the party. The Whips are party members who have the job of making sure that MPs stay loyal to the party. If an MP votes against the party on several occasions or on a very important vote, they may have the 'whip withdrawn'. In other words, they are expelled from the party. In September 2019, the Conservative leader, Boris Johnson withdrew the whip from 21 Conservative MPs for failing to support the party over a vote on Brexit.

Conscience – the MP may have certain religious and/or moral beliefs, which might not allow them to vote for or support certain issues, e.g. to do with abortion, capital punishment, assisted dying, etc.

Pressure groups – will often contact MPs to persuade them to support or oppose something inside or outside of Parliament. The environment pressure group Greenpeace has a guide on its website with ways in which its supporters can try to influence MPs.

National interest – the MP/MSP might have strong views about what is best for the country and they may even disagree with their own party about this (see above examples on Brexit).

Quick Test

1. Between which aspects of their job must an MP divide his or her time?
2. Select three ways an MP can gain influence in the decision-making process. Outline why each would be beneficial.
3. Describe three ways in which pressures on an MP might affect their actions.

Role of the executive and legislature in the UK

> The UK is referred to as a parliamentary government and as both the executive and legislature work closely together, they can often be confused with one another.

Key features of parliamentary government

A Cabinet meeting

- **Executive and legislature membership overlaps** – the Prime Minister and members of the Cabinet are also Members of Parliament.

- **Legislature can remove the executive** – the government is accountable to parliament and should there be extreme conflict between the two, parliament can propose a vote of no confidence. Prior to 2011, the Prime Minister could dissolve parliament by calling a general election, usually when he or she was most confident of winning the election. However, the Fixed-term Parliaments Act was passed on 15 September, 2011, providing for general elections to be held on the first Thursday in May every five years, although an early election can be called if two-thirds of the Commons agrees- as it did when Boris Johnson called a 'snap' election that took place in December 2019.

- **Elections to parliament lead to the formation of the government** – a political party that wins an overall majority in the House of Commons at a general election forms the new government and its leader becomes Prime Minister. If no party wins a majority of the seats then the largest party may form a minority government or there may be a coalition government of two or more parties (see examples above).

Forming an Executive

The Prime Minister appoints ministers who work in the government departments, the most senior of these sit in the Cabinet. This affords the Prime Minister a significant amount of power – 'hire and fire' – Boris Johnson on succeeding Theresa May as Prime Minister 'fired' several Cabinet members, including Trade Secretary Liam Fox and Karen Bradley the Northern Ireland Secretary, replacing them with his own appointments, such as Priti Patel as Home Secretary, who had previously been 'fired' from the Cabinet by Theresa May.

Ministers and MPs

Government ministers are chosen from MPs and Lords in Parliament. Ministers must regularly respond to oral and written questions from MPs and Lords as part of the government being held accountable for their actions. In July 2019, the Secretary of State for Environment, Food and Rural Affairs was asked questions about climate change and plastic pollution. You can see the timetable of upcoming questions here: https://publications.parliament.uk/pa/cm/cmfutoral/futoral.htm

Scrutiny of the government

Parliament checks the work of the government on behalf of UK citizens through investigative Select Committees and by asking government ministers questions. The House of Commons also has to approve proposals for government taxes and spending.

Government bills

Each year the government informs parliament of its plans for new legislation in the Queen's Speech. New legislation is usually introduced in the form of a bill that must be debated and approved by parliament before it can become an Act of Parliament – the government needs the support of the majority of the House of Commons to function.

If a government has a small majority or is working in a coalition, they may rely on MPs from other parties supporting the bill. Otherwise, the government may face defeat and the bill will fail.

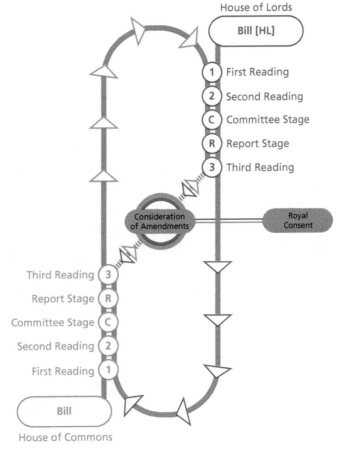

The rigorous process applied for a bill to become a law

TOP TIP

For a detailed account of the relationship between the legislature and the executive, watch MP Andrew Lansley's Open Lecture here: https://www.youtube.com/watch?v=6z1oha_aer4.

Quick Test

1. Why is it correct to suggest that the executive and legislature 'overlap'?

2. What two problems do winning political parties face when forming a government, if they have no majority after a general election?

3. List three difficulties that the executive faces when introducing new legislation.

The Scottish Parliament

The role and influence of MSPs

When the Scottish Parliament was established in 1999, it was founded on the principles of sharing power, accountability, access and participation and equal opportunities. The role and influence of MSPs in the Scottish Parliament go some way to ensuring that these principles are upheld. However, at times the influence that MSPs have could be said to be limited.

MSPs are able to debate and vote on relevant and current devolved matters. They are also able to debate and discuss reserved matters but they are unable to make any amendments to laws regarding these matters.

First Minister's Question Time (FMQT)

FMQT is held each Thursday for 30 minutes and MSPs are given the opportunity to question the First Minister on specific, current topics and hold him or her to account for the actions taken by the government. The FM in this situation has to outline/justify the policy plans, proposals and decisions of the government. The influence MSPs can have, however, is limited by the time – 45 minutes only allows for a maximum of six questions and furthermore the first two questions are afforded to the leaders of the main opposition parties. There have been times when not all six questions tabled have been asked, causing frustration for backbench MSPs.

First Minister's Question Time

Question Time/Themed Question Time

Question Time is held once each week allowing members the opportunity to direct questions to any member of the Scottish Government. Themed Question Time gives MSPs the opportunity to ask questions on a particular theme, so long as it is a devolved matter. It allows members to scrutinise the government and ministers responsible for certain departments. Furthermore, it allows MSPs the chance to ask questions on behalf of their constituents. However, MSPs are entered into a ballot in order to ask a question and are randomly selected by the Presiding Officer. All questions are submitted beforehand in order for ministers to prepare an answer. The final constraint here is that there are usually 10–20 questions on the agenda but MSPs are faced with the issue of time once again, with QT given 20 minutes and TQT given 40 minutes.

Members' Bills

MSPs can introduce a Member's Bill with the aim of it becoming law. Each MSP has the opportunity to introduce two bills per parliamentary session and requires the support of 11 other MSPs. The Presiding Officer decides if the proposed bill falls within the remit of the Scottish Parliament and, once accepted, it must be treated like an Executive Bill,

going through the three stages for passing such legislation. There are limits to how much influence an MSP can have in this area due to the fact that they may require the support of opposition parties to move the bill to the second stage.

Case Study – Repeal of the Offensive Behaviour at Football Act

In April of 2018, the Scottish Parliament voted to repeal the Offensive Behaviour at Football and Threatening Communications (Scotland) Act 2012. This was as a result of a Member's Bill introduced by Labour MSP James Kelly.

Committees

Committees play a central part in the work of the parliament and have often been regarded as its 'engine room'. Committees are cross-party, set their own priorities, independent of government, and are responsible for scrutinising legislation, taking evidence from witnesses and conducting inquiries. Committees can request members of the Scottish Government to attend and give evidence on specific areas of concern, along with members of the public, specialist organisations or pressure groups. Furthermore, they look at the need for new legislation and MSPs are able to establish a committee on a short-term basis to consider particular issues – Private Bill Committees look at a particular

Muriel Gray, chair of the board of governors for the Glasgow School of Art, giving evidence about the Art School fire to the Culture Committee

bill that has been introduced by an MSP. Committees are often asked to review petitions passed from the Petitions Committee if the matter falls into their jurisdiction; for example, in June of 2018 the Education and Skills Committee was asked to consider a petition 'Calling on the Scottish Parliament to urge the Scottish Government to change the law to ensure that musical instrument tuition is available as of right to all children attending state schools in Scotland who wish it, free of charge.' Finally, committees can propose their own bills to parliament; some have been very successful, ultimately becoming law. In 2014, The Children and Young People (Scotland) Act strengthened the rights of children and encouraged all public bodies and government departments to consider how their actions affected the rights of children.

Quick Test

1. List the founding principles of the Scottish Parliament.
2. Outline how an MSP can exert influence with regard to introducing a Member's Bill. Give evidence to support your answer.
3. Watch this short clip on the work of the Health and Sport Committee: https://www.youtube.com/watch?v=FQoNsxR8nUk. Describe the ways in which the committee gathers evidence to help it to carry out its function of 'scrutinising' the government. Give some specific examples from the video.

The Scottish Government

After a Scottish Parliament election, a First Minister is formally nominated by the elected members of the Scottish Parliament and appointed by the Queen, in her capacity as Head of State. Once appointed, the First Minister appoints Scottish government ministers in order to establish a Cabinet, responsible for the different areas devolved to the Scottish Parliament.

First Minister

Since the creation of the Scottish Parliament, Scotland has had five First Ministers.

1. Donald Dewar, May 1999 – October 2000
2. Henry McLeish, October 2000 – November 2001
3. Jack McConnell, November 2001 – May 2007
4. Alex Salmond, May 2007 – November 2014
5. Nicola Sturgeon, November 2014 – present

First Minister of Scotland, Nicola Sturgeon

Role and powers of the First Minister

The role and powers of the First Minister are set out in Sections 45 to 49 of the Scotland Act 1998.

- Since its re-establishment in 1999, there has only been one occasion when a single party has had an overall majority of the MSPs in the Scottish Parliament and was able to pass legislation without having to rely on the support of other parties. The SNP after the 2011 election had an overall majority, whereas the first two elections in 1999 and 2003 produced a Labour / Liberal Democrat coalition, while the 2007 and 2016 elections resulted in an SNP minority government.

- To nominate ministers to sit in the Scottish Cabinet and junior ministers to form the Scottish Government. They can also remove them from office. In 2018, Nicola Sturgeon 're-shuffled' her Cabinet, which saw Jane Freeman replace Shona Robison as Health Secretary and Humza Yousaf became the first Scottish-Asian Cabinet secretary, taking over from Michael Matheson as Justice Secretary. She also expanded the Cabinet from 10 members to 12, including the appointment of Mike Russell with responsibility for government business and constitutional relations covering Brexit and relations with the UK government.
- Responsible to the Scottish Parliament for his/her actions and the actions of the overall Scottish Government.
- Responsible for the development, implementation and presentation of government policy, constitutional affairs and promoting and representing Scotland.
- Delivering oral statements to the Scottish Parliament – at the beginning of each parliamentary term, the FM is able to deliver the government's priorities for the forthcoming term.

The Scottish Government

The Scottish Government is the executive branch of the devolved government of Scotland and operates on the basis of collective responsibility. This means that all decisions reached by ministers, individually or collectively, are binding on all members of the government. Furthermore, the Scottish Government is accountable (answerable) to the Scottish Parliament.

There are nine Cabinet Secretaries (Cabinet Ministers) including the First Minister, and 10 ministers who report to a Cabinet Secretary. Including the two law officers (Lord Advocate and Solicitor General for Scotland), this makes a total of 21 ministers.

Cabinet portfolios
The Cabinet Secretaries have responsibility for the following areas:
- First Minister
- Education and Skills
- Justice
- Health and Sport
- Finance, Economy and Fair Work
- Environment, Climate Change and Land Reform
- Rural Economy
- Government Business and Constitutional Relations
- Communities and Local Government
- Culture, Tourism and External Affairs
- Transport, Infrastructure and Connectivity
- Social Security and Older People

TOP TIP

Use this link to find out more about ministerial roles and responsibilities: www.gov.scot/About/People/Ministers

Relationship with Westminster

In May 2019, the Scottish Affairs Committee of the House of Commons published a report entitled 'The relationship between the UK and Scottish Governments' in which it was stated that the relationship between the Scottish and UK governments had undergone 'significant change in the 20 years since devolution' and that the relationship between the Scottish and UK governments 'has come under renewed strain, after the UK voted to leave the European Union in 2016 and has been characterised by mutual distrust and

First Minister Nicola Sturgeon greets Prime Minister Boris Johnson

political stalemate'. According to the report, several areas of 'tension' between the Scottish and UK governments remain, including:

Brexit: the votes in Scotland and the UK were markedly different, with Scotland voting 62% for Remain while England voted 53.4% Leave.

Indyref 2: the SNP continue to demand a second referendum on Scottish independence because, they argue, the Brexit vote constituted a 'material change' in Scotland's circumstances since the independence referendum of 2014. The UK government refuses to sanction a second referendum.

According to the report, some UK government departments 'lacked the necessary skills and knowledge of devolution to work effectively with the Scottish government or to be fully aware of the impact of UK policies on Scotland'.

Policy differences: since the Scottish election of 2007, the SNP has been in government continuously, during which time the Westminster government has been either a Labour, Conservative or coalition government. This has led to tensions between the Scottish and UK governments. An example of this is the so called 'bedroom tax', or Spare Room Subsidy, which saw housing benefit being reduced for some council or housing association tenants if they had an unused 'spare' room. The SNP government disagreed with this policy and made available additional funding to 'mitigate' the effects of the policy in Scotland.

TOP TIP

The Joint Ministerial Committee (JMC) is designed to improve cooperation and understanding between the UK and devolved governments. Using this link, briefly summarise how it works: https://www.instituteforgovernment.org.uk/explainers/brexit-devolution-joint-ministerial-committee

Quick Test

1. Summarise the main role and powers of the First Minister.
2. Explain the term 'collective responsibility'.
3. Outline the areas of tension between the Scottish and UK governments according to the Scottish Affairs Committee 2019 report.

Electoral systems: First Past the Post (FPTP)

To ensure that you are confident in this section of the course, you should be able to describe the different voting systems in use in the United Kingdom. You should also be able to evaluate each of the voting systems and the impact each has on election results. The simplest way to do this is to look at each system and its advantages and disadvantages relative to the others, using recent election results to support your knowledge and understanding.

First Past the Post (FPTP)

First Past the Post is used to elect representatives in many countries across the world. After Party List, it is the second most popular worldwide electoral system. It is used in the UK to elect members of the House of Commons, in the USA to elect members to Congress and in Canada and India to elect members of the lower houses.

FPTP is used in single member constituencies where the electorate simply mark a cross on the ballot paper next to their preferred candidate. The candidate with the most votes in each constituency wins. The simplistic nature of FPTP is often cited as being one of the key reasons for retaining it as the electoral system of choice in the UK; however, there are continual calls for it to be replaced with a more proportionate system.

Advantages of FPTP

✓ It is simple to understand – voters mark a cross next to their preferred candidate and the candidate with the most votes wins. It is therefore simple to operate and count, and the result can be established very quickly. In 2019, Newcastle Central announced the winning candidate in the constituency only 1 hour and 27 minutes after the polls had closed. In previous elections, in some constituencies the winner has been declared within an hour of the polls closing. As a result, the electorate will usually have a clear idea by the next morning of which political party will form the next government.

✓ It provides a clear link between the representative and the constituents, ultimately giving more effective and accountable representation. Some MPs establish this relationship over a long period of time and remain as the representative for a number of years; Anne McGuire was the MP for Stirling from 1997 to 2015, for example.

✓ It can produce a strong and stable government. Political parties usually have a majority of seats to exercise control over decision making and can implement their manifesto without the negotiation and compromise often caused by a coalition. It gives the political party the opportunity to deliver the policies they were committed to prior to being elected.

✓ It keeps extremism from entering mainstream politics. First Past the Post makes it far more difficult for smaller, radical parties to gain seats and, therefore, influence; for example, UKIP polled 12.6% of the vote in 2015, yet only secured one seat.

Disadvantages of FPTP

✗ FPTP is often criticised for having a large number of 'wasted' votes: those cast for the losing candidates and those cast beyond the winning margin for the successful candidate.

✗ MPs can be elected with a tiny majority of votes. In North East Fife, Stephen Gethins won the seat in 2017 with 2 votes – the smallest margin in UK electoral history; SNP MP Pete Wishart retained his Perth and North Perthshire seat with a majority of only 21. In marginal constituencies, representatives can often find that more voters actually voted against them than for them. Critics would argue this is not democratic.

✗ The number of seats won by a party is not proportionate to the number of votes gained and it could therefore be argued that we do not get a fair result. Analysis by The Electoral Reform Society showed that in the 2017 general election, the Green Party, Liberal Democrats and UKIP received 11% of votes between them, yet they gained just 2% of seats. In fact, since 1935, for approximately 90% of the time the UK has had single-party 'majority' governments, but on no occasion have they had the support of a majority of voters.

> **TOP TIP**
>
> Follow the link: https://www.theguardian.com/politics/ng-interactive/2019/dec/12/uk-general-election-2019-full-results-live-labour-conservatives-tories to find out your MP's majority in the 2019 election.

✗ FPTP can lead to tactical voting as voters will often not vote for their preferred candidate if they don't think they have a chance of winning. They might instead vote for the candidate that they believe has the best chance of beating the candidate they most dislike.

Proportional voting systems applied to 2017 election

Following the 2017 general election, the Electoral Reform Society calculated the effect different proportional representation voting systems would have had on the result. The table below demonstrates how the Alternative Vote, Additional Member System and the Single Transferable Vote would have affected the share of seats compared with the actual result using the First Past the Post system.

> **TOP TIP**
>
> Using the Electoral Reform Society website https://www.electoral-reform.org.uk/voting-systems/types-of-voting-system/ take structured notes on at least two voting systems other than First Past the Post.

Party	Vote %	Seats	Seats %	Alternative Vote	Additional Member System	Single Transferable Vote
Conservative	42.4	318	48.9	304	274	282
Labour	40	262	40.3	286	274	297
SNP	3	35	5.4	27	21	18
Lib Dem	7.4	12	1.8	11	39	29
DUP	0.9	10	1.5	-	-	-
Sinn Féin	0.7	7	1.1	-	-	-
Plaid Cymru	0.5	4	0.6	2	4	3
Green Party	1.6	1	0.2	1	8	1
UKIP	1.8	0	-	0	11	1
SDLP	0.3	0	-	-	-	-
UUP	0.3	0	-	-	-	-
Others	1	1	0.2	-	-	-

2017 General Election results

Quick Test

1. Summarise the key advantages and disadvantages of First Past the Post.
2. Using the Electoral Reform Society table, describe the impact different voting systems might have had on the outcome of the 2017 election.

Electoral systems: the Additional Member System (AMS)

The Additional Member System is a hybrid system that combines elements of both First Past the Post and the Party List. Each constituent is given two votes, one to elect an individual constituency representative and the other to vote for a specific party for a larger region of the country. The political parties will have already preselected a list of potential candidates for this area. In Scottish Parliament elections for example, constituents in Stirling will vote for an individual to represent them in the constituency and they will also select a party who they wish to represent them on the larger regional level of Mid Scotland and Fife, these are the Additional Members.

In the Scottish Parliament, the constituency ballot is used to elect the 73 constituency members, with the second vote allowing constituents to elect the 56 regional members – seven from eight different regions, totalling 129 MSPs.

SCOTTISH PARLIAMENT CONSTITUENCY: NAME OF CONSTITUENCY

VOTE FOR ONE CANDIDATE ONLY

●	**SURNAME** **Forename** Candidate's address Party description	
●	**SURNAME** **Forename** Candidate's address Party description	
●	**SURNAME** **Forename** Candidate's address Description	
●	**SURNAME** **Forename** Candidate's address Party description	
●	**SURNAME** **Forename** Candidate's address Description	
●	**SURNAME** **Forename** Candidate's address Party description	

Scottish Parliament Region: Name of Region

Mark one X only of the paper

Put x in one box ▼

● **PARTY A** (First candidate, second candidate, third candidate, fourth candidate, fifth candidate, sixth candidate, seventh candidate)	
● **PARTY B** (First candidate, second candidate, third candidate, fourth candidate, fifth candidate, sixth candidate, seventh candidate)	
● **PARTY C** (First candidate, second candidate, third candidate, fourth candidate, fifth candidate, sixth candidate, seventh candidate)	
● **PARTY D** (First candidate, second candidate, third candidate, fourth candidate)	
● **PARTY E** (First candidate, second candidate, third candidate, fourth candidate, fifth candidate, sixth candidate, seventh candidate)	
INDIVIDUAL CANDIDATE'S SURNAME **Forename** Description	
INDIVIDUAL CANDIDATE'S SURNAME **Forename** Description	

An example ballot paper used in an AMS election

Advantages of AMS

✓ It retains the accountability of constituency representation with the added bonus of proportionality through the additional members. The results should also be generally proportional with fewer votes being regarded as wasted.

✓ It gives smaller parties a chance of representation in the Scottish Parliament. Not all voters in Scotland support the large, established parties. Since the first election for the Scottish Parliament in 1999, the AMS has allowed success for the Greens, Scottish Socialist Party (SSP) and independents. The Green Party actively campaign on the second ballot rather than spend time fielding constituency candidates who are unlikely to win.

✓ AMS will usually produce coalition or minority government. Four of the five elections so far to the Scottish Parliament witnessed this – 1999 and 2003 saw a coalition formed between Labour and the Liberal Democrats and 2007 and 2016 saw the SNP form minority governments. This promotes political debate, negotiation and compromise.

✓ It allows voters a greater choice. A voter can 'split their ticket' – supporting a candidate in the constituency vote from one party and using the regional ballot to vote for a different party or an independent candidate.

Disadvantages of AMS

✗ It appears to create two different kinds of representative – one for the constituency, who was elected as an individual and is directly accountable, and another who was elected under the guise of their party. The status of the additional members is often called into question as it has been suggested that they owe their seat more to the party placing them high on the list rather than being elected for their individual merits.

✗ By keeping an element of First Past the Post, true proportionality is not achieved.

✗ Parties become more powerful than voters. Political parties will exercise a great deal of control over the regional lists and potential candidates may well see party loyalty and support as the key to success rather than being truly supportive and accountable to constituents.

✗ AMS can often result in a government no-one voted for. The coalitions in the Scottish Parliament between 1999 and 2007 allowed the Liberal Democrats, who had actually came fourth in the election, to hold the balance of power. They were rewarded with senior positions in the Cabinet and many of their policies were implemented as a result of the compromise and debate. In 2019, in order to pass the budget, the minority SNP government was forced to agree a deal with the Green Party to increase tax-raising powers for local councils.

Party	Constituency Seats	Regional Seats	Total Seats	Net Change In Seats +/−
Scottish National Party	59	4	63	−6
Scottish Conservatives	7	24	31	+16
Scottish Labour	3	21	24	−13
Scottish Green Party	0	6	6	+4
Scottish Liberal Democrats	4	1	5	-
Independents	0	0	0	−1

Scottish Parliament election results 2016

TOP TIP

Use the Scottish Parliament website's education section at www.scottish.parliament.uk/visitandlearn/education.aspx to get the most up-to-date information and election results.

Quick Test

1. Summarise how the Additional Member System works in Scotland.
2. What evidence is there from the table that for some parties in Scotland, the regional seats are more important than constituency seats?
3. Outline three advantages and three disadvantages of the Additional Member System.

Electoral systems: Single Transferable Vote (STV)

STV is another form of proportional representation (PR) used in the UK – in Scotland STV is used in elections to local government, and in Northern Ireland it is used to elect local government, Members to the European Parliament and the Northern Ireland Assembly.

How STV works

In practice, representatives are elected from multi-member constituencies/wards. In Scotland, constituents are voting to elect three or four council members to each local council ward. It is a system of preferential voting, so each constituent ranks the candidates in order of preference, meaning placing a '1' next to their most desired candidate, a '2' next to their second most desired and so on.

A quota of votes would be established, using what is known as the Droop quota:

$$Votes\ to\ win = \left(\frac{Valid\ votes\ cast}{Seats\ to\ be\ filled\ +\ 1} \right) + 1$$

If any candidate achieved this quota with first preference votes (FPVs) then he/she would automatically be elected. The surplus votes of the winners would be redistributed to those who did not reach the quota. If not enough candidates have reached the quota, the candidate with the lowest number of votes is eliminated and all of their votes are passed to the next preference on the ballot papers. This process repeats until either a winner is found for every seat or there are as many seats as remaining candidates. This ensures that a voter's preferences on the ballot paper determine how the votes are distributed. No votes appear to be wasted using this system.

Election for Aberdeen City Council
Bridge of Don Ward

Mark the figure '1' opposite the name of the candidate who is your first choice then mark the figure '2' opposite the name of the candidate who is your second choice and so on. You can mark as many choices as you wish but you must number them in order.
Do not mark your ballot paper with an 'X' or a '✓' or any other mark or symbol

INDEPENDENT	**Canavan, Dennis** 14c Love Lane, Linford, LN1 4PD	
INDEPENDENT	**MacDonald, Margo** 12 Grafton Grove, Bromham, AB12 3CD	
SCOTTISH CONSERVATIVE AND UNIONIST PARTY	**Goldie, Annabel** 55 Camellia Crescent, Linford, LN8 3DK	Scottish Conservatives
SCOTTISH CONSERVATIVE AND UNIONIST PARTY	**McLetchie, David** 94 Highland Grove, Bromham, AB18 9QR	Scottish Conservatives
SCOTTISH GREEN PARTY	**Baird, Shiona** 9 Heaven's Gate, Clifftop, LN16 4XS	
SCOTTISH LABOUR PARTY	**Jamieson, Cathy** 16 Thames Close, Bromham, AB13 4EF	Labour
SCOTTISH LABOUR PARTY	**McConnell, Jack** 24 Wallace Walk, Linford, LN4 9BY	Labour
SCOTTISH LABOUR PARTY	**Peacock, Peter** 6 South Africa Road, Horwood, N1 3FG	Labour
SCOTTISH LIBERAL DEMOCRATS	**Stephen, Nicol** 25 Trebor Road, Horwood, N1 9TV	
SCOTTISH LIBERAL DEMOCRATS	**Wallace, Jim** 6 South Road, Biglown, KL1 3FG	
SCOTTISH NATIONAL PARTY	**Lochhead, Richard** 70 Rock Close, Bromham, AB21 12WX	
SCOTTISH NATIONAL PARTY	**Sturgeon, Nicola** 6 Sea Grove, Horwood, N1 6MN	
SCOTTISH NATIONAL PARTY	**Swinney, John** 6 Post Office Grove, Biglown, KL1 6MN	
SCOTTISH SOCIALIST PARTY	**Fox, Colin** 386 Burns Drive, Linford, LN5 7RF	Scottish Socialist Party

An example ballot paper used in a STV election

Case study: Anytown Ward

These are the results for the local elections in Anytown Ward on 5 May 2017:

Valid ballots	**3297**	
Positions to be filled	**3**	
Quota	**825**	(3297 / (3+1)) + 1

Stage 1 first preferences

Clare Bradley	1133	Elected and surplus votes transferred (Stage 3)
David Eddie	34	
Alistair Wilson	1236	Elected and surplus votes transferred (Stage 2)
James Moore	165	
Daniel Clarke	187	
Mark Hunter	157	
Eileen Bristow	385	

It took another four stages before Eileen Bristow was elected.

TOP TIP

Look on the website of your own local authority to find the election results from 2017. The Transfer Report will help you understand the number of stages it took for your councillor to be elected. The link below will take you to the results for the Paisley Northeast and Ralston Ward in Renfrewshire Council: http://renfrewshire.gov.uk/article/4870/Ward-03--Paisley-Northeast-and-Ralston

Advantages of STV

✓ Voters are able to rank candidates from within the same party, which allows voters to judge the candidates on their beliefs, opinions and past voting records. Due to its preferential nature, the system also allows voters to vote across parties, perhaps for an independent candidate who is campaigning on a single issue about which they feel strongly. Following the 2016 local elections in Scotland there were a total of 173 Independent or non-aligned councillors, which is more than Liberal Democrats and Greens combined.

✓ Due to the surplus votes being redistributed, voters feel like all votes count and none are wasted, giving a highly proportionate result. In 2017, the SNP won 32.3% of the first preference votes, giving them 431 seats, with the Conservatives gaining 25.3% of FPVs and 276 seats, and Labour with 20.2% of FPVs won 262 seats.

✓ Voters have a choice of representatives to whom they can take their issues. Within the Hillhead Ward of Glasgow City Council, each voter has a choice of four representatives, representing three different parties: SNP, Labour and Green.

Disadvantages of STV

✗ Multi-member constituencies are often criticised for weakening the positive link formed between individual MPs and constituents under FPTP.

✗ The degree of proportionality for less popular parties is often criticised. In 2017, the Green Party secured 4.1% of the first preference votes but only gained 19 seats, which is 1.5% of the total.

✗ Coalition governments are likely to occur. The results in Scotland after 2017 left 29 local authorities from a total of 32 with no single party in overall control. In fact, none of the 32 councils were won outright by any of the major parties. As a result, there are a large number of local authority administrations being run by minority or coalition administrations; for example, the SNP and Labour parties have entered into coalitions to run Edinburgh City and Stirling councils.

Quick Test

1. Summarise the key advantages and disadvantages of Single Transferable Vote.
2. What feature of STV gives it a high level of proportionality?
3. What difficulties might local authorities face if there is no single party with overall control? You could try to find an example of where this has been a problem to support your answer.

Electoral systems: Party List

Party List is a further form of PR, which is used in Israel and countries throughout Europe. It has been used in Scotland, England and Wales to elect members to the European Parliament (as well as being the format for electing the Additional Members to the Scottish Parliament).

How MEPs are elected

When this book was being revised, the UK had not left the European Union, therefore the following may no longer apply to the UK; however, the process as explained below will apply to any election using the same version of the Party List as used in the UK to elect MEPs.

The UK was divided into 12 electoral regions, each electing a number of MEPs (between three and 10). In total, the UK had 73 MEPs representing it in the European Parliament.

The UK used a 'closed list' where voters simply vote for a party rather than an individual. Parties select the candidates list themselves and are allocated seats in proportion to the number of votes they achieve, using a mathematical method called the D'Hondt formula. Candidates at the top of each party list are more likely to be elected than those further down.

The UK's 12 electoral regions

Advantages of Party List

✓ Voting could not be simpler – each voter has one vote for either one party or an independent candidate.

✓ A higher degree of proportionality is more likely than when using FPTP, although there can still be a degree of dis-proportionality. For example, in the EU election of 2019, while the Labour party gained 13.7% of the votes and 13.7% of the seats, the Brexit Party with 30.5% of the vote won 39.7% of the seats. Overall, however, the 2019 results in the UK were broadly proportional.

✓ Closed lists make it easier for women and ethnic minorities to be elected. In 2014, 41% of MEPs elected in the UK were women and in 2019 this increased to 49%.

Disadvantages of Party List

✗ As a result of proportionality, many smaller parties and sometimes more extreme parties can gain power. This could lead to instability. In the 2014 European Parliament election, UKIP came top in the election in the UK. Previous to this, the BNP had won two seats in the 2009 election (they lost both in 2014).

✗ The close link between constituents and representatives formed under FPTP does not exist. People in Scotland have a choice of only six MEP representatives in total.

✗ As with the AMS, political parties become more powerful than voters. Any party member who is likely to deviate from the party line will be unlikely to feature high on the list.

TOP TIP

Use this link to visit the website of the Electoral Reform Society and take notes on the different types of List systems used around the world: https://www.electoral-reform.org.uk/voting-systems/types-of-voting-system/party-list-pr/

Quick Test

1. Identify the key features of the Party List electoral system.
2. Summarise the main advantages and disadvantages.

Voting behaviour: social class

Psephologists (political scientists who study elections) continue to analyse how individuals in society interact with politics. They do this in the hope that they will be able to draw conclusions about the nature of voting patterns and political parties would, therefore, be able to predict where to target their campaigning. However, over the years it has become evident that voting behaviour is shaped by both short- and long-term influences and it is often difficult to make conclusions about overall patterns of voting behaviour. We do know, however, that there are key factors that influence voting behaviour. (For analysis of voting patterns and trends in the 2019 general election, see 'Election Update' on pages 78–87.)

Social class and the electorate

Analysis of voting behaviour began in 1945 using an individual's socio-economic status. At this time, groups A, B and C1 were traditionally Conservative supporters while social classes C2, D and E voted Labour. This was mainly due the political parties' ideas meeting the needs of each of the groups, e.g. Conservatives believed in limited government interference while Labour championed the redistribution of wealth. Over time, class has appeared to be less influential and the idea of **class dealignment** grew in importance. There is clear evidence of this in more recent elections, see the table below.

	Class AB voters	Class C1 voters	Class C2 voters	Class DE voters
2001				
Conservative	39%	36%	29%	24%
Labour	30%	38%	49%	55%
2005				
Conservative	37%	37%	33%	25%
Labour	28%	32%	40%	48%
2010				
Conservative	39%	39%	37%	31%
Labour	26%	28%	29%	40%
2015				
Conservative	45%	41%	32%	27%
Labour	26%	29%	32%	41%
2017				
Conservative	47%	44%	45%	38%
Labour	37%	40%	41%	47%

Source: Ipsos MORI

It could be argued that this continued shift in voting behaviour occurs as a result of political parties adopting a more 'catch-all' approach to their policies, in order to attract the highest number of voters. However, we have to consider other factors that might impact on how citizens vote. This 'loosening' of social class and party voting is evident in the results of the 2017 election in which, according to Ipsos MORI 'The middle classes swung to Labour, while the working classes swung to the Conservatives'. Although the Conservatives still had more ABC1 votes than Labour, the swing to Labour in this social class was 12%. Similarly, Labour was still stronger among traditional working class voters; however, the Conservatives saw a 12-point swing to them from C2DEs.

Issue-based voting undoubtedly affects how people vote and will often be more important than social class in determining how people vote. In 2017, the British Electoral Survey showed that voters felt that Brexit was 'by far' the most important issue facing the country.

Over time, class has appeared to be less influential on voting behaviour

TOP TIP

Use the following link to gain further information relating to factors that affected voting behaviour in 2019: https://yougov.co.uk/topics/politics/articles-reports/2019/12/17/how-britain-voted-2019-general-election

Quick Test

1. Why do psephologists continue to analyse voting patterns in the UK?
2. Using the results table, analyse the changes that have occurred with regard to voting and social class between 2001 and 2017.
3. Using the internet, compare the policies of the three main political parties in the 2017 general election and identify three policies that could be described as 'catch-all'.

Voting behaviour: geographical location

Does where you live influence how you vote?

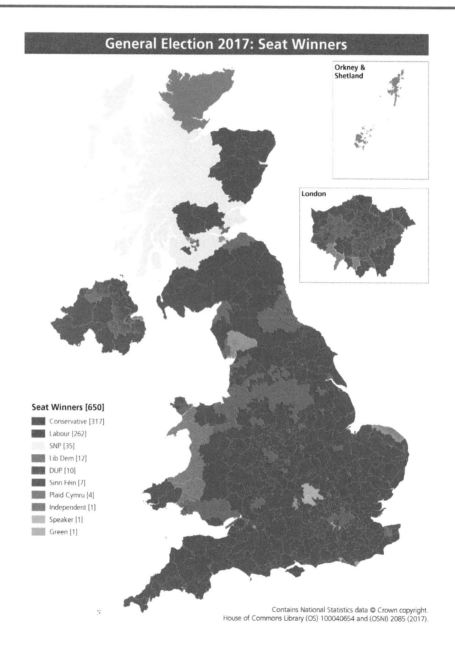

General Election 2017: Seat Winners

Orkney & Shetland

London

Seat Winners [650]
- Conservative [317]
- Labour [262]
- SNP [35]
- Lib Dem [12]
- DUP [10]
- Sinn Féin [7]
- Plaid Cymru [4]
- Independent [1]
- Speaker [1]
- Green [1]

Contains National Statistics data © Crown copyright.
House of Commons Library (OS) 100040654 and (OSNI) 2085 (2017).

Traditionally, support for the two biggest parties, Conservative and Labour, tended to be stronger in particular areas, with Labour being strongest in the north of England, Scotland, Wales and the old industrial areas, while the Conservatives tended to draw their greatest support from the south of the UK as well as suburban and rural areas – the so-called 'North–South' divide. While this remains true to some extent, as we shall see, there have been significant changes in recent years.

As is evident from the map of the 2017 UK general election, the Conservatives dominated in the Midlands, the east of England and the south and south west. They also made significant gains in Scotland where they improved their representation from 1 to 13 MPs. In 2017, the Labour Party was strongest in the north of England, Yorkshire and Humberside, Wales and London. In Scotland, which until fairly recently had been a stronghold for them, Labour added five seats to give them a total of six. In the 2015 election they had almost been 'wiped out' by the SNP, leaving them with only one MP in Scotland. The Scottish National Party dominates elections for both the Scottish and UK Parliaments in Scotland. In the 2015 Westminster election, the SNP won 56 of Scotland's 59 Westminster seats, although this fell to 35 in the election of 2017. Plaid Cymru (Party of Wales) has never won any more than 4 of the 40 Welsh seats in Parliament.

Clearly then there are still regional and national patterns of voting in the UK; however, as we will see below, these 'traditional' patterns are being wakened by other factors including the UK's relationship with the EU, Scottish independence and the weakening of social class ties to the 'big two' parties, Conservative and Labour.

Political parties pay great attention to regional support, as due to the way FPTP voting works they can often focus their election campaigns in specific areas, hoping to win a number of marginal constituencies. For example, in the 2019 election, the Liberal Democrats targeted North East Fife, the most marginal seat in the UK. The constituency had a higher than average remain vote in the EU referendum and the Lib Dems campaigned on their pro-EU policy in the hope of winning the seat. They won the seat from the SNP's Stephen Gethins, overturning a two-vote majority to beat Mr Gethins by a majority of 1,316.

Quick Test

1. Explain what you understand by the 'North–South divide'.
2. Why do political parties pay an interest in regional support during elections?
3. North East Fife was the most marginal seat in the UK in 2017, with an SNP majority of 2. Explain why the Lib Dems targeted this seat in particular.

Voting behaviour: age

Age and voting behaviour

Age appears to be a significant influence on voting behaviour and can have an impact on elections. In fact, according to Ipsos MORI, in the election of 2017, 'Age was an even more dividing factor than in 2015 (and the biggest we've seen since our records began in 1979)'. Various explanations have been given for this, such as different age groups having different life experiences – the older the voter, the more loyal they may be to a particular party (in the period 1992–2017, the over-50s in general favoured the Conservatives). As the YouGov table shows, voters in the 18 – 49 age group were more likely to vote Labour; while the Conservatives were strongest in the over-50 age group. Although there was an increase in voter turnout among young people in 2017, they were still less likely to vote than older people; for example, only 57% of 18–19 year olds voted compared with 84% of people over the age of 70.

TOP TIP

Visit the websites of Ipsos MORI, YouGov and the British Election Survey to research current levels of support for the main parties by age group.

Age and the 2017 general election

The table below highlights how the UK voted by age in 2017

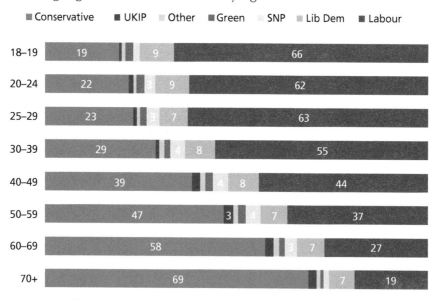

Source: YouGov

The table above clearly shows that younger people favoured Labour and older people favoured the Conservatives in 2017. An analysis of age-related voting in 2017 showed that for every 10 years older a voter is, they are about 9% more likely to vote Conservative. The so-called 'tipping point' where people are more likely to vote Conservative and less likely to vote Labour has been calculated at 47.

Scottish independence referendum

In 2014, younger voters played a key role in the referendum because 16 and 17-year-olds were entitled to vote. More than 109,000 younger voters were registered to vote, apparently voting in favour of independence. The Lord Ashcroft Poll suggested that 71% of 16–17-years-olds voted Yes with 29% voting No (however, the poll had a very small sample size). However, YouGov's final poll of 3188 voters showed that 51% of those aged between 16 and 24 voted No.

Should we link age to other factors such as issue voting? MORI polls would suggest that at times issues can play a more important role for younger voters than the party leader or party policies. In the 2014 referendum, the key issues affecting voting appeared to be the NHS, currency, defence and the EU. In the 2017 general election, the main issues influencing voting behaviour were Brexit, terrorism, the NHS, immigration and the economy. However, issues change over time and are regarded as short-term influences that are often a reflection of the political climate.

Younger voters played a key role in the referendum

Quick Test

1. What evidence is there that 'age is the biggest dividing factor' in the 2017 election?
2. Why are issues regarded as short-term influences in relation to voting behaviour?

Voting behaviour: gender

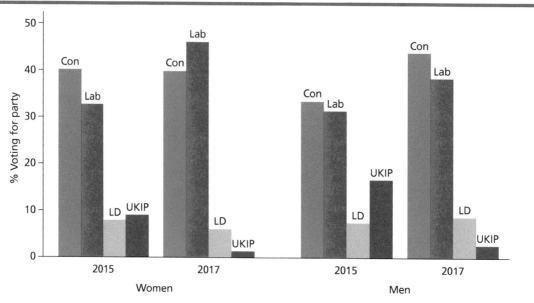

Vote by gender in 2015 and 2017

As the British Election Study graphs above show, male and female votes can vary from election to election; however, there are some general patterns that can be observed over time. In terms of rates of participation in elections, the turnout of male and female voters is broadly similar, although surveys by polling organisations suggest that women are more likely to say they are 'undecided' in the run-up to elections. Political parties are, of course aware of this and will 'target' women during the campaign. In 2015, Labour ran their Women to Women campaign and in 2017, each of the manifestos of the main parties included policies that were more likely to attract female voters such as enhanced childcare and improved employment rights for women returning to work after having children. It is, however, misleading to suggest that the 'pattern' of gender voting is fixed over time; for example, between the 2015 and 2017 elections women 'flipped' from being more likely to vote Conservative to being more likely to vote Labour in 2017.

In recent elections and in the 2014 Scottish independence referendum and the 'Brexit' referendum of 2016, a number of differences can be seen in the way in which women and men voted and participated. There were significant gender differences within certain age groups: in 2015 and 2017, women under 25 were more likely to vote Labour than men in the same age group. In the 66 and above age group, women were more likely to vote Conservative than men, while in 2015 and 2017, support was higher for UKIP among men. In the Scottish independence referendum of 2014, men voted 53% 'Yes', while women were 57% for 'No' and in the EU referendum in 2016, 55% of men voted leave while 49% of women voted leave.

It is sometimes claimed that women are less likely to be actively engaged in politics than men; however, a House of Commons Briefing Paper in 2019 showed women made up 47% of the membership of the Labour Party, 46% of the Green Party, 43% of the SNP, 37% of the Lib Dems and 29% of the Conservative party. This is a significant improvement when compared with previous years and the 2019 election saw this trend continuing with a record number of female MPs elected.

More recently, we have witnessed all-women shortlists in elections and a number of political movements developing, such as the formation of 'The Women's Party' and 'Women for Independence', highlighting the continued interest in gender-specific politics. This will continue to keep politicians interested in courting the female vote in forthcoming elections.

TOP TIP

Look at the manifestos of the main political parties prior to the 2017 UK election. Identify policies that are aimed at gaining the female vote.

Quick Test

1. Explain why political parties will 'target' the female vote during election campaigns.
2. Describe the changes in male and female support for the parties between the 2015 and 2017 elections.

Voting behaviour: ethnicity

Evidence suggests that ethnic minority voters are far less likely to vote and less likely to be registered to vote than white voters; for example, in the 2017 election, voter turnout among Black, Asian and minority ethnic (BAME) voters was estimated to be around 59%, compared with 70% for whites. In 2015, turnout among BAME voters was even lower at around 53% compared to 67% for white voters (House of Commons Briefing Paper, June 2019). This is attributed to a number of reasons.

Labour and ethnic minorities

Encouraging ethnic minorities to vote has been a problem for a number of years. People from ethnic minority groups often believe that their vote will make little difference. This has been partially due to the high concentrations of ethnic minorities in safe Labour seats, where poverty and deprivation are common. Although support for the Labour Party has decreased slightly in recent elections, the 2017 election showed that ethnic minorities are still much more likely to vote Labour than Conservative, with 77% voting Labour. According to the Runnymede Trust, in 2017, ethnic minority voters made up 1 in 5 Labour voters but only 1 in 20 Conservative voters.

Conservatives and ethnic minorities

The Conservative Party in particular has realised that it needed to attract support from ethnic minorities. This was seen in the period before the 2015 election when government ministers attended community events and places of worship in constituencies with significant ethnic minority populations. Minority group MPs were promoted to the Cabinet and several policies were announced to appeal to minorities, including targets to increase the number of BAME people in work, university, the police and armed forces. In the 2015 election, the Conservatives received over 1 million BAME votes for the first time. In 2017, Theresa May spoke of the 'burning injustices' facing many minorities and her 'Race Audit' highlighted the extent of inequalities facing minority groups in the UK. There are of course different ethnic groups within the BAME communities and there are differences in the way they vote. British Indians, especially Hindus, for example, are more likely than those from an Afro-Caribbean background to vote Conservative. Between 2010 and 2017, the Conservatives increased their support from this group from 30% to 40%. Even among Black British Africans there was a small increase from 11% to 14%. It is suggested that as more people from these backgrounds move into professions and to the suburbs, they are more likely to regard Conservative policies as more relevant to them.

Ethnic minority representation

In the 2017 election, a record number of 52 MPs were from ethnic backgrounds, accounting for 8% of the total; however, ethnic minorities make up around 13% of the UK population. In the 2017 election, 10% of Labour candidates and 7% of Conservative candidates were from ethnic backgrounds, although both parties were much more likely to put forward these candidates for constituencies with higher than average ethnic populations. Thus, the trend is an improving one; however, minorities are still under-represented.

Quick Test

1. What evidence is there to show that minorities are less likely to vote than white people?

2. Describe the efforts the Conservative Party has taken to encourage ethnic minorities to vote for them.

3. 'There has been no improvement in recent years in the level of representation of minorities in UK politics.' How true is this?

The impact of the mass media on voting behaviour: television

There is great debate as to how influential the media can be. On the one hand, it could be argued that the mass media simply reflect as well as reinforce political preferences that are already established. However, it could also be argued that the mass media are able to distort the flow of political information by setting the agenda for debate and transmitting information when and how they see fit, easily manipulating the voting intentions of the undecided.

Television as mass media

Despite the rapid growth in social media in recent years, for the majority of the population TV is still the most widely used form of media. In 2017, research carried out by YouGov, on behalf of the London Press Club and Society of Editors, showed that 'traditional' sources of news such as newspapers and TV were still more influential than social media, with 60% of people saying they regularly got their political news from broadcasters, especially the BBC and newspapers such as the *Guardian* and the *Daily Mail*. It follows that most people's main source of political information is television news broadcasts and current affairs programmes. In the days prior to any election, there is extensive TV coverage of the campaign and this has huge potential to shape political attitudes, given that TV is still the favoured and trusted source of information for the majority of the population. This may be due to the fact that TV is regulated (TV coverage should be impartial); however, all political parties have complained about the BBC at some point. Politicians and political parties use TV to promote a positive image, with sound bites being carefully planned and speeches reduced to concise statements to be more easily quotable.

Memorable slogans were used during the Brexit campaign, which featured prominently in TV coverage

The rise of the TV debate

In 2010, TV debates were held between the three main party leaders, with 9.9 million viewers tuning in to the first debate. In this first debate it was Liberal Democrat leader Nick Clegg who emerged the overall winner. The first substantial poll, conducted by Populus, for *The Times* found Clegg the overwhelming winner with 61% and Cameron and Brown trailing on 22% and 17% respectively.

In 2010, the Liberal Democrat vote went up 1% overall in the UK; however, they lost five seats, so it could be argued that the debates and the popularity of Clegg made no difference. David Cameron and the Conservatives managed to maintain a positive image – TV helped perhaps and they increased their share of the vote by 3.8%, gaining 97 seats. Labour lost 91 seats and decreased their share of the vote by 6.2%. Could we argue therefore that this was a combination of TV influence and a poor image of the party leader?

In 2015, more than a third of voters were said to have been influenced by the TV debates. A Panelbase survey found 38% were influenced by the debates, 23% by TV news coverage and 10% by party political broadcasts. In April 2015, an average audience of 7 million viewers watched the leaders debate on ITV, the only live debate in which David Cameron took part. The survey further highlighted the power of TV with only 25% stating newspapers had been influential in helping form their opinions compared with the 62% who stated TV as being most influential. Websites at 17% and radio at 14% proved insignificant in comparison.

Before the 2014 referendum on Scottish independence, two debates took place involving Alex Salmond, leader of the SNP and Alistair Darling who was arguing for a 'No' vote. ICM polls after the debate showed that viewers thought Alisatair Darling 'won' the first debate with Alex Salmond doing better in the second; however, polling expert Professor John Curtice of Strathclyde University stated that the debates had little or no effect on people's voting intentions.

In the 2017 campaign, Theresa May chose not to take part as she felt campaigning 'on the doorsteps' was more effective.

Quick Test

1. What evidence is there to show that TV is still regarded as influential in shaping voting behaviour?
2. According to Professor Curtice, to what extent did the debates before the independence referendum influence people's voting intentions?
3. In what ways might political parties 'present' their polices in order to reach a TV audience?

The impact of the mass media on voting behaviour: newspapers

Newspapers can have great influence, given that they play an important role in providing political information. Newspapers are not neutral, they decide which stories are covered and how they are covered, and are often clearly in favour of one party or another and are inclined to switch support over time. As a result, they are in a powerful position to influence public opinion and will often take credit for securing victory for a party.

Newspapers' political allegiances

In 1997, the *Sun* famously backed Tony Blair and the Labour Party, the predicted winners of that year's election. However, by September 2009 they ran a front page headline stating 'Labour's Lost It', highlighting the end of their support for the Labour Party. Following on from that, in 2010 they printed a front page in the style of the 2008 US Obama campaign, showing support for David Cameron and the Conservatives – significantly by this point the Conservatives were already ahead in the opinion polls. In the 2017 election they urged their readers 'Don't put Britain in the Cor-Bin', referring to the Labour leader Jeremy Corbyn, and listing on the front page the 'threats' to Britain they said a Corbyn government would bring.

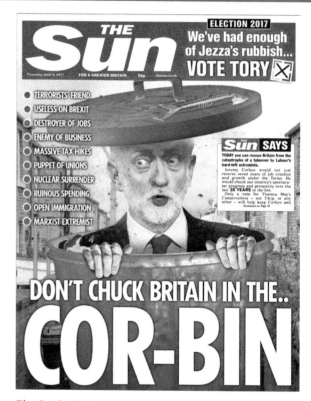

The Sun's 2017 cover

When considering newspaper readership and voting patterns, there is evidence that suggests influence. A total of 68% of those reading the *Daily Mirror* in 2017, a clear supporter of Labour, voted Labour, with 79% of *Telegraph* readers voting Conservative. However, we have to consider again whether this could be a simple reinforcement of pre-existing opinions.

In 2007, the *Scottish Sun* supported the Labour party in the run-up to the 2007 Scottish Parliament election, yet the SNP won the largest number of MSPs and formed a minority government. By 2011, the *Scottish Sun* supported the SNP and their share of MSPs increased significantly, allowing them to form a majority government.

In recent years, there has been growing concern about the influence that the press can exert over political parties. It is argued that political parties have actively courted the press, showing their recognition of its influence. However, there is a danger that the ownership of the media is concentrated in too few hands and as a result they are able to shape public opinion and influence voting behaviour. This was further evidenced in 2015 when the *Scottish Sun* supported the SNP, yet in the rest of the UK the *Sun* supported the Conservatives. The lack of impartiality may lead to a loss of trust among readers. Although the table below clearly shows that only three of the ten national newspapers in the UK were more likely to have Labour supporting readers than Conservative, it is important to remember that surveys have also shown that the newspapers that backed a political party only reinforced their readers' choice – they were going to vote that way anyway – than persuaded their readers to change their minds and switch parties. It is also important to remember that around 40% of readers are unable to say which party their newspaper of choice supports.

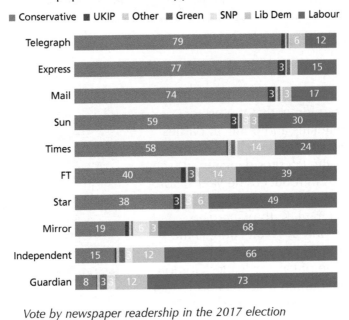

Vote by newspaper readership in the 2017 election

Quick Test

1. What is the key difference between newspapers and TV with regard to political coverage?
2. What evidence is there that newspapers can have an impact on their readers' voting behaviour?
3. What evidence is there that newspapers have limited impact on voting behaviour?

The impact of the mass media on voting behaviour: internet and social media

In recent years we have witnessed an immense growth in the use of the internet and social media by both political parties and politicians in an attempt to influence voting behaviour. The web acts as a key source of information and a valuable method of communication for all involved. Political party websites, political blogs and forums, 24-hour news online, YouTube and social media networking sites such as Facebook and Twitter have been actively used in order to engage the general population in politics.

Facebook and Twitter as political tools

It is sometimes easy to forget that the use of social media by politicians and political parties is actually fairly new. When President Obama launched his bid for the US presidency in 2007, Twitter had only been introduced the year before, although this election was described as the first 'internet election'. In the UK, the *Guardian* newspaper described the 2010 election as the first social media election, referring to the fact that Sarah Brown (wife of Labour leader Gordon Brown) had over one million followers on Twitter and more than 100 MPs were reported as using Twitter to communicate with the electorate.

Smartphones make it easy to access political information online

Certainly, by the time of the 2017 election all political parties and the majority of candidates were using social media to get their message across. Figures produced by the Electoral Commission after the 2017 election showed that between them, the main parties spent about £40m on Facebook, with the Conservatives spending the most with around £18.5m while Labour spent just over £11m. There are, however, some questions about whether social media is actually reflecting the public's views or actually influencing them. Analysis by YouGov and the British Election Survey of the use of social media by the Labour and Conservative parties in 2017 suggests that rather than changing people's minds, social media was more likely to reinforce views already held – for example, the most 'shared' messages during the campaign were amongst the so-called 'Corbynistas' or supporters of Labour leader Jeremy Corbyn. What is more, it was found that even though many people, especially younger people, get most of their news from social media, the sources they trusted most on social media platforms were organisations like the BBC and newspapers such as the *Guardian* and the *Daily Mail*.

Social media and the 2019 EU election

Although there is some doubt about the effectiveness of social media in changing people's minds, the use of social media in the 2019 election for the European Union, which was dominated by 'Brexit', would suggest that a single issue, simple message can be effective in reinforcing already held views. According to the *Guardian* newspaper, in the campaign for the 2019 European Union elections, the Brexit Party accounted for 51% of all shared content even though it was only responsible for creating 13%. As outlined in the previous section, content is most likely to be 'shared' among people with similar viewpoints. The Brexit Party

The Brexit Party used social media effectively in the 2019 EU election campaign

was described as having 'simpler, stronger messaging and a deeper understanding of their audience' with 39% of all ads focused on attacking Labour being sent to older users of Facebook in England, rather than younger voters or people in Scotland and Northern Ireland.

Foreign interference in UK politics

In recent elections and referendums in the UK and elsewhere, there has been concern expressed about attempts by foreign governments to influence the outcome of elections using social media. In a 2019 report by the UK Parliament entitled 'Disinformation and fake news', it was stated that 'There has been clear and proven Russian influence in foreign elections, and we highlighted evidence in our Interim Report of such attempts in the EU Referendum.' As evidence, the report referred to research by organisations including Cardiff University and 89UP. This interference took the form of 'fake' Facebook accounts, adverts paid for by foreign governments or people working for them, so-called 'propaganda farms' in foreign countries that have posted millions of negative Tweets about elections and referendums in the UK.

> **TOP TIP**
>
> You can read more about foreign interference in UK politics here: https://publications.parliament.uk/pa/cm201719/cmselect/cmcumeds/1791/179109.htm

Quick Test

1. What evidence is there to show the importance of social media in UK politics?
2. Why can it be argued that social media 'reinforces' existing views more than it changes people's views?
3. What methods have been used by foreign governments to try to influence the outcome of elections and referendums in the UK?

Election 2019 – Update

Background

On 29 October 2019, MPs in the House of Commons voted to hold an early election. This was the result of many moths – in fact years – of disagreement about the United Kingdom's withdrawal from the European Union following the 2016 referendum (see elsewhere in this topic). There were deep divisions among the parties in the Commons about how, and even if, the UK

Party	Seats won	% of vote
Conservative	365(+47)	43.6%(+1.2)
Labour	203(−59)	32.2%(−7.8)
Lib Dem	11(−1)	11.5%(+4.2)
SNP	48(+13)	3.9%(+1.1)
Green	1(0)	2.7%(+1.1)
Voter turnout	67.3%(−1.5)	

Results of the UK General Election (2017 results in brackets)

should withdraw. Not surprisingly, the election was dubbed in the media as the 'Brexit Election'.

The outcomes of that election were very significant, with some major changes to the electoral map of the UK. In his post-election analysis, the polling expert, Sir John Curtice, Professor of Politics at Strathclyde University, made the following points:

- The Conservatives won a large majority of 80 seats due to a large swing from Labour to the Conservatives in the areas that voted leave in the European withdrawal referendum.
- The exception was Scotland where the SNP almost 'swept the board' with 48 seats from a total of 59 Scottish seats in Westminster.
- Labour had its worst result since the 1930s, while the Conservatives had their biggest victory since Margaret Thatcher's win in 1987.
- Conservative support increased by an average of 6% in 'Leave' constituencies but fell by 3% in 'Remain' constituencies.
- Labour's vote fell by 10 points in the most 'Leave' constituencies but it also fell by over 6 points even in pro-'Remain' constituencies.
- Labour lost a lot of seats in its traditional working-class heartlands; for example, in the north-east of England and Yorkshire, where its vote fell by over 12 points.
- Support for the Lib Dems actually increased, although they gained one seat less than 2017.
- Despite being described as one of the most important elections in recent years, slightly fewer people voted than in 2017.
- The election was dubbed the 'Brexit election' but more than half of the votes went to pro-'Remain' parties.

Regional changes

Traditionally, the Labour Party dominated the old industrial areas of the north of England, Wales and Scotland. So strong was Labour in the north of England, these seats were sometimes described as Labour's 'Red Wall'. As the maps below show, many of the constituencies in the 'Red Wall' elected Conservative MPs – some for the first time ever in their history. In Scotland, where the SNP have won more seats than any other party in the last three UK elections, they once again dominated with 48 out of 59 Scottish seats while the Labour Party returned only one MP. This is a dramatic change since 2010, when Labour won 41 seats to the SNP's 6.

How Britain voted in 2017 and 2019

What would the result have been if Proportional Representation had been used?

The Electoral Reform Society recalculated the result of the election to show what would have happened if the UK had used the same voting system in the general election as it used for elections to the European Parliament. According to this, the Conservative Party would not have had an overall majority and would have had 77 fewer seats, while the Labour Party would have gained 10 more. The party that seemed to suffer most from the First Past the Post system was the Liberal Democrats who would have had 59 more seats under this PR system while the Brexit Party, which did not win any seats at all, would have won 10 seats. The most likely result then would have been another 'hung' parliament.

In Scotland, PR would also have produced significantly different results.

Party	Seats won	If PR used
SNP	48	27
Conservative	6	15
Lib Dems	4	6
Labour	1	11

How PR would affect Scottish seats

The independence question - Indyref 2

As explained elsewhere in the text, the SNP have stated their intention to demand a second independence referendum, arguing that the vote to leave the EU in 2016 was against the wishes of the Scottish people. This, they argued, was a 'material change of circumstances' that justified Indyref 2. The SNP leader, Nicola Sturgeon, stated that by gaining 48 of Scotland's 59 Westminster seats in the election, the SNP had a 'mandate' to hold a second referendum. Prime Minister Boris Johnson, however, confirmed his opposition to this, saying the result of the 2014 independence referendum 'should be respected'.

Women and minorities in Parliament

The 2019 general election resulted in a record number of women being elected. In total, there are now 220 female MPs from a total of 650. Despite this improvement, women still only make up 34% of MPs and there are quite significant differences between the parties. While the Labour party will now have more women MPs than men, less than a quarter of Conservative MPs are female and the SNP has twice as many male as female MPs. The Liberal Democrats have the highest proportion of female MPs but this is from a total of only 11. The election also saw an increase in the number of BAME MPs from 52 in 2017 to 63, representing 9.5% of the Commons. This compares with the 19.5% of the UK population who are recorded as BAME. Labour has the largest number of minority MPs with 39. Of the 32 members of the Cabinet appointed by the Prime Minister after the election, there are 6 from BAME backgrounds and 8 women.

TOP TIP

Although it is too early to tell how important social media was in the election, visit the website Who Targets Me: https://whotargets.me/en/party-spending-race/ to see how much each party spent on social media during the 2019 campaign.

Voting by age, gender and social class

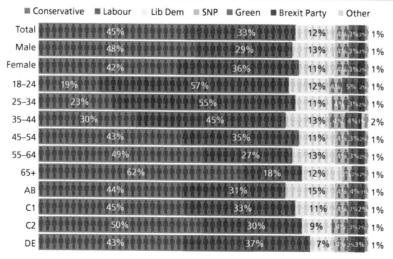

Voting by age, gender and social class – Lord Ashcroft Poll

As you can see from this poll conducted by Lord Ashcroft immediately after the election, Labour did better among younger voters in the 18–34 age group, while the Conservatives dominated all other age groups – people were more likely to vote Conservative the older they were. The graph also shows the extent to which Labours 'traditional' working-class support (C2 & DE) voted in large numbers for the Conservatives. Many Labour voters, who had never voted for anyone other than Labour, 'switched' to the Conservatives in this election. Again, Professor Curtice comments: 'The bond between Labour and its traditional working-class base is now badly strained'. Men were much more likely to vote Conservative than Labour with a gap of 19% while women were also more likely to vote Conservative but with a gap of only 6%.

The main issues of the election

It is without doubt that the main issue of the 2019 election was Brexit as can be seen by how people voted in 'Leave' and 'Remain' constituencies; however, it was not the only issue affecting how people voted, with the supporters of some parties giving more importance to certain issues than others.

Issue (%)	ALL VOTERS	CON	LAB	SNP	LIB DEM
NHS & hospitals	55%	41%	74%	57%	58%
Getting Brexit done	36%	72%			
Stopping Brexit	21%		28%	43%	65%
The economy and jobs	21%	29%		18%	17%
Climate change	16%		20%	19%	30%
Poverty & inequality			27%	24%	12%
Having the right leader		25%			
Spending cuts			22%		
Immigration		24%			

How Britain Voted and Why

Quick Test

1. Using the information on voting trends in both the 2107 and 2019 elections, describe some of the main changes between the two elections.

2. What evidence is there to suport the view that the 2019 election was the 'Brexit election'?

Participation

How do citizens participate in the UK?

UK citizens are able to participate in a number of different ways. For the majority of UK citizens, **voting** will be their main form of participation. Citizens are able to vote in a number of different elections:

- UK general election
- Regional elections to the Scottish Parliament, Welsh Assembly and the Northern Ireland Assembly
- Local government elections
- European Parliament elections
- Referenda
- By-elections

Turnout at these different elections is variable, highlighting that citizens are not consistent in their levels of participation.

Turnout rates

Turnout at these recent elections has been variable:

- UK general election 2017   68.8%
- Scottish Parliament election 2016   55.6%
- European Parliament election 2019   36.9% (EU average = 50.62%)
- Scottish independence referendum 2014   84.5%
- EU referendum 2016   72.2%

In some areas of the UK, citizens may also be able to participate in more specific elections such as those to elect the London Mayor or the London Assembly. However, there are a huge number of opportunities for participation in addition to voting.

Methods of participation

Some methods of participation include:

- Standing as a candidate.
- Joining a political party.
- Becoming a member of a pressure group.
- Supporting a political campaign (e.g. canvassing on behalf of a candidate, leafleting, phone bank).
- Submitting an e-petition.

GOT IT? ☐ ☐ ☐

> ## Case study: e-petitions (https://petition.parliament.uk)
>
> Online petitions, or e-petitions, are a straightforward way of allowing UK citizens to influence government decision making. Citizens can submit an e-petition on anything for which the UK government is responsible. If the e-petition acquires at least 100,000 signatures it will be considered by the Backbench Business Committee for a debate in the House of Commons. On a number of occasions, e-petitions have gone as far as being debated on the floor of the House of Commons; for example, in April 2019 the petition to revoke Article 50 (i.e. to cancel Brexit) which had over 6 million signatures, was debated as was the petition in 2017 that called for a ban on President Trump making a state visit to the UK.
>
> **TOP TIP**
>
> Visit the Scottish Parliament website at www.scottish.parliament.uk to find out the types of petitions being submitted in Scotland.

Quick Test

1. For the majority of UK citizens, what is their main form of participation?
2. Could citizens participate more in elections? Give evidence to support your answer.
3. Research a further e-petition and assess whether it had any impact or influence on government decision making.

Pressure groups

Pressure groups (interest groups) are groups of like-minded people who have come together as a result of their similar values and opinions. It is their intention to either bring about change or prevent change occurring and by joining or supporting a pressure group, citizens aim to influence the political decision-making process, on either a local, national or international level. There is a huge range in the size, type and variety of pressure groups, with some having been established for a lengthy period of time and others existing only until the change they are campaigning for has occurred.

Rights and responsibilities of pressure groups

Pressure groups have certain rights and responsibilities when attempting to influence the decision-making process. They are free to inform the general public of their values and opinions and are able to campaign using a significant number of methods. However, alongside this pressure groups should also maintain high levels of respect for other citizens and organisations and ensure that their campaign methods remain legal.

The following rights and freedoms are protected in the UK by the Human Rights Act:

- Right to peaceful protest/freedom of assembly.
- Freedom of expression.
- Right to publicly criticise the government.

In addition, pressure groups have the following responsibilities:

- Information given to the public must be accurate and not damage a person's or organisation's reputation.
- Protests should be carried out in a peaceful, legal manner.
- Pressure groups should not slander anyone or any organisation – this breaks defamation laws and the pressure group may be sued.

Methods used by pressure groups

Pressure groups attempt to attract attention to their cause by gaining widespread media publicity. Different pressure groups use different methods, ranging from simple petitions to more extreme publicity stunts. In June of 2019, 14 members of Greenpeace were arrested when they used their ship *Arctic Sunrise* to block the route of an oil rig heading out to North Sea oil fields.

The Greenpeace banner at Mount Rushmore

Other methods used by pressure groups may include:

- Demonstrations
- Publicity campaigns (leaflets, posters, online advertisements)
- Lobbying MPs/MSPs/councillors
- Mass/social media campaigns
- Public meetings
- Hiring professional lobbyists

Characteristics of different pressure groups

Insider (e.g. BMA, Age UK)	Outsider (e.g. Greenpeace, Extinction Rebellion)	Cause (e.g. RSPCA, PETA)	Interest (e.g. National Union of Journalists)
• High profile • Regarded by government as legitimate • Strong links with decision makers • Regularly consulted • Long-term political influence	• Work outside of government • Fewer opportunities to influence directly • Adopt different strategy to insider groups • Can be radical • Can be ideologically opposed to political system	• Promote particular cause or value • Not self-interested • No formal restrictions on membership • Can rely on member donations	• Promote particular interests • Aim to benefit their own members • Membership from particular sector • Fee paying

Case studies: pressure group success stories

Fans Against Criminalisation

In an effort to tackle sectarian behaviour at football games in Scotland, the Scottish government passed the Offensive Behaviour at Football and Threatening Communications (Scotland) Act in 2012. Supporters groups, in particular Fans Against Criminalisation, organised protests and petitions and lobbied MSPs in order to voice their objections against the Act, which they felt singled out football fans unfairly. Many MSPs who opposed the Act had taken into consideration the points made by Fans against Criminalisation and the Act was repealed in April of 2018, which the Fans Against Criminalisation called 'a historic victory for football fans'.

The British Medical Association

In 2019, the British Medical Association (BMA) campaigned against the changes to the tax laws applying to the pensions of senior doctors in England. Some senior doctors including hospital consultants and senior GPs refused to work overtime as it was affecting how much they would get in their pensions. This action was partly blamed for rising waiting lists. Following consultations between the government and the BMA, the tax rules were changed. Dr Chaand Nagpaul, of the British Medical Association stated that 'After tireless lobbying…it is good to see the government finally sitting up and taking notice'.

TOP TIP

Ensure that you are familiar with the aims of at least one local, national and international pressure group, focusing on their key successes and the methods they use to exert influence.

Quick Test

1. Outline what a pressure group is trying to achieve. Use the case studies to support your answer.

2. Do the methods that some pressure groups use go against their democratic rights and responsibilities? Give evidence to support your answer.

3. Based on the table of characteristics of pressure groups on page 85, which group would the following belong to? You may have to conduct some online research to help you decide:

- British Medical Association
- Fire Brigade Union
- Greenpeace
- Stirling Before Pylons
- Child Poverty Action Group
- Oxfam
- Fathers for Justice (F4J)
- National Farmers' Union
- CND

What is inequality?

> *'Inequality is the difference in social status, wealth, or opportunity between people or groups.'*
>
> *The Collins Dictionary definition of inequality*

Inequalities in income and health

The definition given above highlights that inequality relates to a **difference** in size and circumstance. In the UK, when referring to inequality we can easily identify this difference with regard to the **wealth** and **health** of UK citizens.

Income inequalities have been increasing over a number of years with the poorest 10% of the population seeing a decrease in their incomes. Alongside this, the richest 10% of the population have seen significant rises in their income. The *Guardian* newspaper ran an article on wealth inequality in the UK in May 2019 that quoted figures from the Resolution Foundation suggesting that the richest 1% in Britain owned between 14 and 20% of the nation's wealth. The reason they were unable to be more definite was, according to the Foundation, the lack of information available about the top 1%. In 2018, the Institute for Public Policy Research estimated that the top 20% of households earned six times more than the bottom 20%.

Wealth is often held by the select few

Alongside income inequality, the poorest in the UK appear to suffer the poorest health. In May 2019, Public Health England figures showed that the gap between life expectancy in the richest and poorest areas 'has significantly widened between the years 2011 to 2013 and 2015 to 2017 to 9.4 years for males and 7.4 years for females'. It also showed that the gap in healthy life expectancy was 19 years. Although other recent surveys found a reduction in the total number of people engaging in 'risky behaviours' – smoking, excess alcohol use, poor diet and a sedentary lifestyle – the type of people who were stopping smoking or drinking less were mainly in the higher socio-economic and educational groups. Further health inequalities are evident in Scotland, where a Scottish Government report highlighted that men and women in the most deprived communities can expect to spend 22.7 and 26.1 years respectively in 'not good health'. These examples are clear indicators that inequality exists in the UK.

Quick Test

1. What two key indicators can be used to assess inequality?
2. What evidence is there that the rich are getting richer and the poor are getting poorer?
3. What are the 'risky behaviours' that will undoubtedly impact on your health?

Evidence of inequalities in the UK

Poverty

Poverty is a key indicator that inequalities exist in the UK. Poverty can be measured in a number of ways: Peter Townsend, a sociologist and one of the founders of the Child Poverty Action Group, defined poverty as 'when they [families/individuals] lack resources to obtain the type of diet, participate in the activities and have the living conditions and amenities which are customary, or at least widely encouraged and approved, in the societies in which they belong'.

Poverty can be measured in a number of ways

There are many different ways to measure poverty. The most commonly recognised measure is that households earning less than 60% of the median income are considered to be living in poverty. Since 2015, the UK government has used a different measure that some groups have said could be misleading. Organisations such as the Child Poverty Action Group use figures produced by the Social Metrics Commission (an independent 'think tank' on measuring poverty) which, in 2018, showed that around 22% of the UK population were in poverty (58% of whom were in 'persistent poverty') and nearly 33% of children were in poverty. It also showed that poverty rates were 'not much different' from 2000 but there had been a significant fall in pensioner poverty.

Socio-economic status

Recent evidence would suggest that there is a widening gap in wealth inequalities between those in the higher occupational classes and those in the lower occupational classes. In 2018, the Office for National Statistics (ONS) report on household income inequality showed that the richest fifth of the population saw a 4.7% rise in average income while the poorest fifth saw an average reduction of 1.6%. This, according to the ONS, was a reversal of the trend in recent years that saw a reduction in income inequality; however, the gap between the richest and poorest in 2018 was only slightly lower than before the financial crisis in 2007. It would appear from the ONS report that only limited progress has been made in reducing income inequality. The Equality Trust in 2018 showed that the poorest fifth of society have only 4% of the total income, whereas the top fifth have 47%. In 2018, the World Economic Forum placed the UK 11th out of 25 countries for income inequality.

TOP TIP

You can look at the Equality Trust's findings in detail here: https://www.equalitytrust.org.uk/scale-economic-inequality-uk

The BBC conducted a major survey entitled 'The Great British Class Survey' that suggested people in the UK now fit into seven categories, using measures of not just economic and social capital but also cultural capital. The seven categories identified were:

1. Elite
2. Established middle class
3. Technical middle class
4. New affluent workers
5. Traditional working class
6. Emergent service workers
7. Precariat, or precarious proletariat

> **TOP TIP**
>
> For further information on poverty in the UK, visit the website of the Office for National Statistics and search for 'poverty'.

This further highlighted inequalities between different groups in society when considering earnings, occupation, education, housing tenure, social interactions and geographical location.

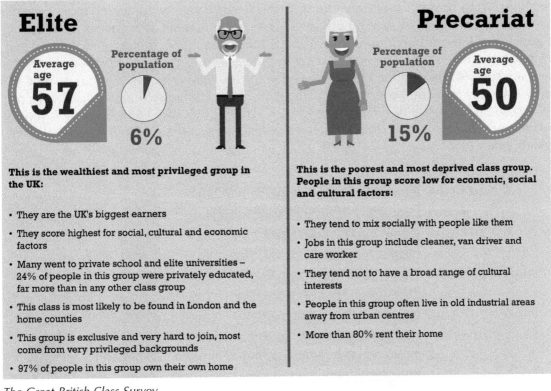

Elite

Average age **57**

Percentage of population **6%**

This is the wealthiest and most privileged group in the UK:

- They are the UK's biggest earners
- They score highest for social, cultural and economic factors
- Many went to private school and elite universities – 24% of people in this group were privately educated, far more than in any other class group
- This class is most likely to be found in London and the home counties
- This group is exclusive and very hard to join, most come from very privileged backgrounds
- 97% of people in this group own their own home

Precariat

Percentage of population **15%**

Average age **50**

This is the poorest and most deprived class group. People in this group score low for economic, social and cultural factors:

- They tend to mix socially with people like them
- Jobs in this group include cleaner, van driver and care worker
- They tend not to have a broad range of cultural interests
- People in this group often live in old industrial areas away from urban centres
- More than 80% rent their home

The Great British Class Survey

The Social Mobility Commission report to Parliament in 2019 showed that a person's class background can have a significant effect on their life chances; for example, it stated that people from better-off backgrounds were 80% more likely to be in a professional job than those from working-class backgrounds and that on average, people from working-class backgrounds earned 24% less than those from better-off backgrounds. This 'social immobility' had not changed in the four years before the report, despite government attempts to improve it.

Further evidence to highlight the major wealth inequalities in the UK is the continued growth in the number of billionaires in the UK alongside the continuing high levels of poverty. The *Sunday Times* 'Rich List' for the UK in 2018 listed 145 billionaires in the UK – the largest number of billionaires proportionate to the population worldwide. London has more billionaires than any other city in the world, while also suffering huge levels of poverty. According to the London Data Store, in 2018 the total number of Londoners in poverty had continued to rise over the last few years to around 2.4 million or 28% of the total population. The poverty rate in London is persistently higher than the national average and in 2018 it was 6% higher, with the highest levels found in Inner London.

What does become evident is that factors causing inequalities are often inter-related, i.e. the lower your socio-economic status, the more likely it is that you will be in poverty. This is further supported in the next section when looking at geographical inequalities.

Geographical inequalities

Inequalities and poverty levels vary across the UK, with poverty appearing more prevalent in the north than the south and in urban rather than rural areas. It is often a reflection of the lack of jobs and opportunities within certain areas and is therefore closely related to socio-economic status. The constituency profiles listed in the table below show that there are specific areas of the country that suffer more than others. London has some of the worst areas for child poverty in the UK, with Tower Hamlets council in east London having the highest child poverty rate in the UK with 56.7%. In 10 constituencies, mostly in London, Birmingham and Manchester, more than half of the children live below the poverty line.

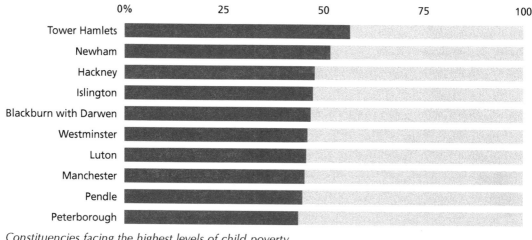

Constituencies facing the highest levels of child poverty

There is further evidence to highlight geographical inequalities in relation to health. Scotland has had the lowest life expectancy in the UK for decades and 2019 figures from the National Records of Scotland (NRS) showed that boys born in the most deprived areas of Scotland, such as Glasgow City, can expect to live 10.8 years less than boys born in more affluent areas such as East Renfrewshire. For girls the difference was 7.5 years. Apart from living shorter lives, children in poor areas of Scotland will suffer more ill health throughout their lives, with boys spending almost one-third of their lives in poor health compared with only 13.1% for a boy born in a more affluent area.

Glasgow in particular suffers higher levels of early death and ill-health compared with cities such as Belfast, Liverpool and Manchester that seemed to have a similar recent history of job losses, poverty, poor diet, etc. Research carried out by the Glasgow Centre for Population Health (GCPH) revealed that Glasgow suffered around 30% more deaths under age 65 than these 'similar' cities. In 2018, the Scottish Public Health Observatory report into 'Excess Mortality in Scotland and Glasgow' stated that the population of Glasgow was more affected than the other cities due to more persistent levels of poverty, poorer housing conditions and overcrowding. They also claimed that government and local councils in Scotland did not effectively tackle the 'root problems' affecting Glasgow.

> **TOP TIP**
>
> To find out more about life expectancy in Glasgow, visit the Glasgow Centre for Population Health website here: https://www.gcph.co.uk/population_health_trends/life_expectancy_in_glasgow

Quick Test

1. How does Peter Townsend of the Child Poverty Action Group define poverty?

2. What evidence is there to suggest that the gap between rich and poor continues to widen?

3. Give evidence to highlight the inequalities that exist in terms of wealth within London; you may want to refer to the information on socio-economic status.

4. Summarise the information on life expectancy in Scotland; is there evidence to suggest that the health of people in Glasgow is poorer than that of those living in other parts of the UK?

Theories of inequalities in the UK

Social explanations/theories

Social explanations of inequality are often related to the hierarchy of power in society and are linked to socio-economic status, gender and ethnicity. Such factors would suggest that those at the higher end of the scale are white, educated and male. Social explanations further highlight that inequality exists in two key areas – inequality of opportunity and inequality of conditions.

- Inequality of opportunity = life chances, that is, health, education, crime.
- Inequality of conditions = income inequalities, that is, wealth, housing, material goods.

There are two main social theories of inequality: functionalist theory and conflict theory.

Functionalist theory

Functionalists would suggest that it is necessary and desirable for inequalities to exist in order for society to survive. They would argue that inequalities exist as a direct result of certain occupations and positions in society requiring a higher level of training, education and expertise and should, as a result, gain greater rewards. According to this view, therefore, society operates as a meritocracy based on ability.

Conflict theory

Conflict theorists would argue, however, that inequality exists due to the dominance of one group in society over another. They would argue that opportunities for social mobility are often difficult due to the repressive nature of those operating at the higher end of society because of their significantly greater political and economic power.

Individualistic/collectivist theories

Individualist theories of inequality would suggest that it occurs as a direct result of the behaviour and lifestyle choices made by the individual. Individualists would argue that it is the responsibility of the individual to prevent themselves and their families from suffering inequality and they would discourage the government from providing too much support, arguing that when too much support is available, individuals will relinquish responsibility and become reliant on welfare. They further argue that lifestyle choices of the individual are a direct cause of wealth and health inequalities, with the individuals who choose to smoke, consume excess alcohol, eat a poor diet and lead a sedentary lifestyle paying the price for those choices. Poor lifestyle choices in turn lead to poor health, which can have a long-term impact on the ability of people to be fit for work. As a result, the gap between those at the higher end of society (rich/affluent) and those at the lower end continues to grow.

Again, there is significant evidence to support this theory; however, what we often see is that the two theories are interrelated, i.e. those making poor lifestyle choices that lead to health inequalities are often doing so as a result of their income inequalities.

Collectivists, on the other hand, believe that it is the government's responsibility to reduce inequalities and to provide for those who are unable to meet their basic needs through poverty, worklessness, ill-health etc. The collectivist argues that services such as education, health and welfare should by provided free at the point of delivery and should be 'collectively' funded through taxation.

Income inequalities

Low paid and part-time workers suffer high levels of poverty. The Joseph Rowntree Foundation reported in 2018 that the number of people living in poverty in working families had risen by over a million in the previous three years. Although the National Minimum Wage rose to £7.70 per hour in 2019 for someone over the age of 21, it is still argued to be less than what is required to meet the cost of living in the UK. In these situations it is often harder to cope financially than being unemployed as some part-time workers may not be entitled to any benefits and find that they are worse off in work. The Living Wage Foundation further highlighted this when they calculated that £9.00 per hour (£10.55 per hour in London) is required to meet the basic cost of living, and they encourage employers to provide this.

This is further evidenced in the 'Health and Wellbeing Survey' carried out by NHS Greater Glasgow and Clyde in 2017/18. The survey found that those living in the poorest areas of Glasgow are still twice as likely to have no qualifications as those in other areas.

Homelessness

The majority of the UK public would acknowledge that employment is the key method to escaping poverty; however, those that are homeless are disadvantaged because they have no corresponding address for employment applications and day-to-day survival is often more of a priority than finding a job.

A homeless man in Edinburgh

TOP TIP

You can find out more about some of the social and economic issues affecting the Glasgow area in the report 'NHS Greater Glasgow and Clyde 2017/18 Adult Health and Wellbeing Survey'

Obesity

According to a 2019 House of Commons Briefing Paper on obesity statistics in the UK, there is clear link between obesity, poverty, educational levels and ethnicity. The study showed that in the most deprived areas of England, people were 11% more likely to be obese than those in the least deprived areas. It was also shown that people with Black ethnicity had the highest levels of obesity while those with no qualifications were 12% more likely to be obese. For children living in the poorest areas of England, childhood obesity was almost twice as high as in the least deprived areas. Childhood obesity rates among 10–11-year-old children in the poorest areas have risen by 5% in the last decade while it is largely unchanged in the least deprived areas.

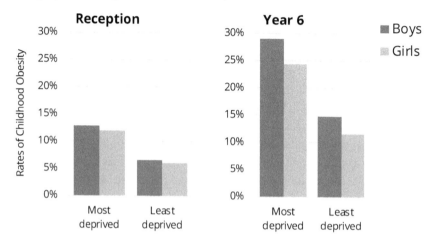

Children living in deprived areas are more likely to be obese than those in less deprived areas

Smoking

NHS Health Scotland identifies smoking as 'the most important preventable cause of ill-health and premature death in Scotland with around 10,000 smoking-related deaths every year'. There is also a strong connection between smoking and inequality. Smoking rates are much higher in the most deprived areas of Scotland with 35% of adults smoking compared with 10% in the least deprived areas. Among pregnant women, almost 30% in the poorest areas smoke compared to less than 5% in the least deprived areas.

Quick Test

1. Explain the difference between collectivist and individualist theories of inequality.
2. List the factors associated with higher levels of obesity.
3. 'Those living in the most deprived areas are more likely to suffer poorer health.' What evidence is there to support this statement?

Impact of inequalities: gender inequalities

Inequality in society can have a devastating impact on a number of people, and these effects can range from a lower income to lower life expectancy. However, there is clear evidence to suggest that some groups suffer greater effects with regard to their wealth and health than others. These groups may include children, the elderly, women and ethnic minorities. This section will focus on the impact of inequality on women and the next section will focus on ethnic minorities.

Gender inequalities: women and work

In 2019, the business organisation PricewaterhouseCoopers (PWC) reported that Scotland had been ranked top of the 12 nations and regions of the UK for representation of women in the workplace. There are five 'indicators' that are used to measure the involvement of women in the workforce: gender pay difference; overall female participation in the workforce; female unemployment rate; female full-time employment rate and the gap between male and female participation in the workplace. In each of these indicators, with the exception of female full-time employment, Scotland was either equal to or ahead of the UK. However, even in work, inequalities exist.

The Office for National Statistics (ONS) in 2018 published figures showing that although the overall gender pay gap had been closing over time and the number of women in full-time work had been increasing steadily since the early 1970s, women on average earned almost 18% less than men. The gap was somewhat smaller for women in full-time work at 8.6%. In 2018, there were approximately 4.7 million low paid workers, 60% of whom were female, and women were much more likely to work part time (41%) compared to men (13%). There are a number of reasons for this.

Women are more likely than men to:

- Work part time
- Work in lower-paid jobs (the so-called '4 Cs' – caring, cleaning, catering, clerical)
- Take career breaks to have and care for children
- Have more responsibility for looking after elderly parents
- Face employer prejudice and discrimination

TOP TIP

Consider the management structure in your own school – is there a gender imbalance? Compare this to your primary school (most primary school head teachers in Scotland are women).

Discrimination

It is argued that sex discrimination, although outlawed by numerous pieces of legislation, continues to exist in the workplace, with women finding it difficult to achieve promotion or managerial/executive positions. For example:

- Women make up only 29% of board directors of FTSE 100 companies.
- The Equality and Human Rights Commission reported to the House of Commons in 2016 that 'three in four mothers (77%) said they had a negative or possibly discriminatory experience during pregnancy, maternity leave, and/or on return from maternity leave'.

Women further find it difficult when trying to break into occupations that would give them a higher profile such as politics and the media.

- As of the 2019 general election, 220 of the 650 MPs in the House of Commons are women.
- The Scottish Parliament (35%) and Welsh Assembly (47%) do better than Westminster.
- The Women in Journalism organisation in 2017 showed that front-page newspaper stories were much more likely to be written by men than women, with the three worst papers being the *Daily Mirror* (10%), the *Sun* (15%) and the *Daily Express* (16%).
- Over half of all those studying law are female but only 14.9% of QCs (top judges) are female.

Women make up only 29% of board directors of FTSE 100 companies

Female health

The ONS reports that females live longer than males but spend more time living with illness or disability. In 2018, Public Health England calculated that women will on average spend at least 3 years more than men in ill health and further evidence highlighted a link between wealth and health in that teenage conception rates are highest in areas of deprivation. Alongside this, NHS Health Scotland acknowledge that although men have a higher suicide rate than women, women are more likely to be admitted to hospital than men from self-harming, and 70% of patients given a diagnosis of 'anxiety or other related illness' by their GP were women. Deprivation is cited as the key factor in the existence of such inequalities.

Life expectancy figures suggest that health is improving, with people living longer. However, the life expectancy gap is an indicator of inequalities suffered by women due to geographical location: women, as well as men, can expect to live a significantly shorter life in certain locations.

Life expectancy

	Male	Female
Dorset	83 years	86.4 years
Glasgow City	72.6 years	78.4 years

Quick Test

1. What evidence is there to support the claim that women in the workforce in Scotland do better than elsewhere in the UK?

2. List the reasons why women, on average, continue to earn less than men.

3. Do women suffer inequalities in relation to health? Give evidence to support your answer.

Impact of inequalities: ethnic inequalities

The 2011 census showed that the number of ethnic minorities living in the UK was an estimated 8 million, 14% of the population, with certain studies projecting numbers to double by 2050. However, when it comes to income, employment, education, housing and health, minorities suffer disproportionate inequality. This can be as a result of numerous factors ranging from prejudice and discrimination to lifestyle choices and deprivation.

Educational attainment

In August 2019, the Department for Education in England published GCSE figures showing that pupils from the Chinese, Asian and Mixed ethnic groups scored higher than average, while White pupils and Black pupils scored lower than average. Pupils from the White Gypsy/Roma and Irish Traveller ethnic groups had the lowest average scores. The number of students gaining degrees by ethnic group highlights the improvement in educational attainment. However, there is vast evidence to suggest that these improvements do not transfer to the workplace.

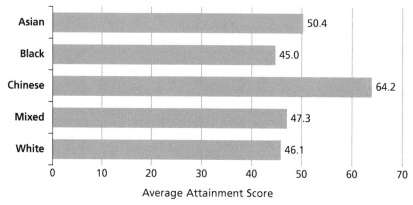

Education attainment by ethnicity

Income inequalities

- Approximately 36% of all ethnic minorities live in low-income households, compared with 17% of the White population.
- There are inequalities within and between ethnic groups. The proportions who live in low-income households are:
  - 30% for Indian and Black Caribbean.
  - 45% for Black African.
  - 55% for Pakistani.
  - 65% for Bangladeshi.

- In all parts of the UK, ethnic minorities, on average, are more likely to have lower incomes than Whites. However, there are greater differences in areas such as inner London, northern England and the Midlands, where high levels of ethnic minorities are concentrated. This is evident in unemployment rates as well as levels of ill health and inadequate housing.
- More than 70% of ethnic minorities living in inner London are on low incomes.

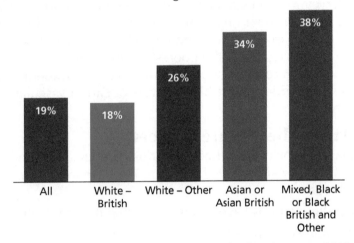

Proportion of people in relative poverty after housing costs, 2013–18

Furthermore, the Scottish Government in 2019 published its estimates for poverty and ethnicity. The figures showed that for the period 2013 to 2018, people from minority ethnic (non-White) groups are more likely to be living in poverty after housing costs are taken into account. Poverty among the White British group was 18%, while the levels for Mixed, Black or Black British was 38% and 34% for those from the Asian or Asian British ethnic group.

Unemployment

Although the level of unemployment in the UK has fallen steadily since 2013, according to the House of Commons Briefing Paper 'Unemployment by Ethnic Background' in May 2019, it is evident that both within and between various ethnic groups there are significant differences in the levels of unemployment. As the graph shows, the gap between White and BAME levels of unemployment, although narrowing, is still significant. Following the economic downturn in 2008, White unemployment peaked at 7.8% while the rate for those from a BAME background peaked at almost double – 14.7%.

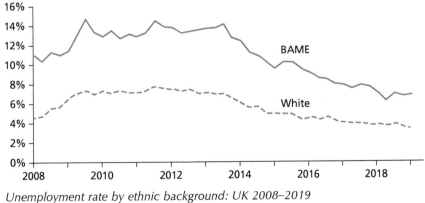

Unemployment rate by ethnic background: UK 2008–2019

Health inequalities

Ethnic minority groups generally suffer poorer health than Whites; however, there are inequalities within and between ethnic groups. The UK government has published data suggesting that income and socio-economic position are the key factors relating to poor health. The Health Survey for England suggested that ethnic minorities report higher levels of poor health and also report poor health at a younger age than Whites. These surveys also indicate that there are variations between ethnic groups, with Pakistani, Bangladeshi and Black Caribbean people reporting the poorest health, while Indians are on a par with White and Chinese people in reporting better health. When considering various illnesses and conditions, ethnic minorities report higher levels of cardio-vascular disease (CVD) but lower levels of cancer.

Case study: uptake of healthcare services

- Government data has shown that ethnic minorities are less likely to access hospital care; for example, South Asians have been found to have lower access to care for coronary heart disease.
- Fewer people in ethnic groups have stopped smoking than in white groups.
- The Healthcare Commission patient surveys have suggested that people from some ethnic groups are less satisfied with NHS services; for example, South Asian patients report poorer experiences in hospitals.

Housing

In 2016, the housing charity Human City Institute published a report on housing and ethnicity. The report showed that ethnic minorities tend to suffer inequalities in housing that subsequently lead to inequalities in health. The report concluded:

BAME groups were much more likely to experience 'housing stress' than Whites. In the two decades before the report, BAME homelessness had grown from 18% to 36%.

BAME households were also far more likely to live in overcrowded, inadequate or fuel-poor housing than Whites.

One in six ethnic minority families had a home with a 'category 1 hazard' that affected health.

There was an over-concentration of BAME households in Britain's most deprived areas. Housing inequality resulted in lower life expectancy and poorer health among minorities.

Securing housing is a concern for all, including ethnic minorities

Quick Test

1. What evidence is there to suggest that the educational attainment of ethnic minorities has improved?

2. Outline the key issues for ethnic minorities in relation to income and employment.

3. In what ways might poor housing affect the health and life expectancy of minorities?

Government response to inequalities

The UK has a long history of providing a comprehensive welfare state in order to protect the social and economic wellbeing of its citizens. This has involved the UK government's Department for Work and Pensions (DWP) and the devolved parliaments in Scotland, Wales and Northern Ireland introducing legislation, providing services in relation to health and education, as well as support given directly to individuals in the form of benefits.

Universal Credit

Universal Credit is a benefit payment for people in or out of work. It was introduced in a few pilot areas in 2013 and is to be rolled out across the whole country. It is replacing or rolling into one single payment some benefits and tax credits that are currently available. The benefits to be replaced include Housing Benefit, Child Tax Credit, Income Support, Working Tax Credit, Jobseeker's Allowance and Employment Support Allowance. The stated aim of the government in introducing Universal Credit was to simplify benefits, make them more efficient and give people more incentive to get into employment. It is paid as a single amount into the claimant's bank account. The payment covers the previous benefits they were entitled to. Claimants are then expected to meet the cost of things like rent from the payment. Claimants of Universal Credit are eligible to work and there is no limit to the number of hours worked – payment of Universal Credit will reduce the more they earn. In the past, people could lose all of a benefit they had been receiving if they worked or earned over a 'threshold' amount. Universal Credit was intended to avoid this 'cliff edge'.

Thérèse Coffey (Secretary of State for Work and Pensions)

In order to receive Universal Credit, the claimant must accept a claimant commitment. This is an agreement that the claimant will do certain tasks, dependant on their health, responsibilities at home and how much help is needed to get to work.

Criticisms

Universal Credit has been heavily criticised by opposition political parties, anti-poverty campaigners and the media as a result of the change to a monthly payment, which claimants often find difficult to manage, and the many technical problems faced during the rollout period. The rollout of Universal Credit took much longer than expected and cost several times more than was expected. As the payments are made 'in arrears', claimants will have to wait 5 weeks to receive their first payment. Many people on Universal Credit are not able to manage their finances very well. Landlords claim there has been a rise in rent arrears as claimants no longer have their rent paid directly to the landlord in some parts of the country.

Benefits

TOP TIP

Use the UK government website to research how the most recent budget will affect benefits allocated to different groups: www.gov.uk/browse/benefits

Unemployed: New Style Jobseeker's Allowance (JSA)

New Style JSA is financial support given to those over the age of 18 who are actively seeking and are able for work. JSA also provides a work coach to help the claimant devise a work plan relating to how they are going to find a job. Claimants must attend a Jobcentre Plus office (usually every two weeks) to 'sign on' and inform the work coach of what they have been doing to seek employment, e.g. job applications and interviews. Failure to comply with the criteria may result in claimants having their JSA stopped.

Unemployed: Employment and Support Allowance (ESA)

Paid to those claimants who are ill or disabled and are unable to work. ESA is seen as personalised support so that there is help available to get the claimant back into work if possible. Claimants must attend 'Work Capability Assessments' while their claim is being assessed.

A Jobcentre Plus office where claimants attend a fortnightly meeting

The assessment establishes the extent to which claimants are unable to work and the amount awarded is dependent on their circumstances. Claimants must attend regular interviews with an advisor to set 'job goals' and look to improve their employability skills.

Low-income families

Working Tax Credit (WTC)

WTC is available to those who are:

- 16–24 and have a child or a qualifying disability
- 25+ with or without children.

Claimants must work a certain number of hours per week but their income must fall below a certain level. It is all dependent on personal circumstances. As of 2019, Working Tax Credit had been replaced by Universal Credit for most people.

Free school meals

Families in England and Wales claiming certain benefits (Income Support, Universal Credit, Child Tax Credit) may be eligible for free school meals for their children. In Scotland, all Primary 1–3 children, no matter the financial situation, are eligible for free school meals. This has affected around 130,000 children with parents saving over £300 a year per child. This is regarded as more than a financial support and is viewed as an attempt by the Scottish Government to improve children's health by providing a nutritious, well-balanced meal each school day.

Child Benefit

Paid to parents as long as they don't have an income of over £50,000. The weekly payment is £20.70 for the eldest or only child, with £13.70 a week paid for each additional child.

Personal Independence Payment (PIP)

Personal Independence Payment (PIP) is available to people aged 16–64. PIP aims to help with the extra costs caused by long-term ill health or a disability. It may also be paid to claimants who need help looking after themselves, have daily living difficulties or have walking difficulties. Daily living difficulties might include:

- Preparing or eating food
- Washing and bathing
- Dressing/undressing
- Reading and communicating
- Managing medicines
- Making decisions about money

The rate paid depends on how their condition affects an individual, not the condition itself. Claimants undergo an assessment to work out the level of support to be given. The rate is regularly reassessed to ensure accurate support is being given and to attempt to avoid benefit fraud.

Elderly

State Pension

This is a regular financial payment once people reach state pension age (the age at which someone receives their state pension will depend on when they were born; state pension age in 2020 is 66 and will rise to 67 by 2028 and 68 by 2046). Pensioners can receive up to £168.60 per week, depending on previous income and National Insurance contributions made. However, the government guarantees households a minimum income. To make up the difference between the State Pension and the minimum income guarantee, pensioners can apply for other benefits to top up their state pension, including Pension Credit.

Elderly benefit payments include the State Pension

Winter Fuel Payment

An annual payment of between £100 and £300 tax-free to help pay for heating bills. Most payments are made automatically between November and December and if the claimant receives the State Pension they should automatically be sent a Winter Fuel Payment.

Other benefits

The following benefits may be available to different groups (although many of these will eventually be replaced by Universal Credit):

- Income Support
- Housing Benefit
- Council Tax Benefit
- Free bus travel
- Child Tax Credit
- Sure Start Maternity Grant
- Cold Weather Payment
- Education Maintenance Allowance

Benefit cap and the two-child limit

As part of the UK government's 'austerity measures', they introduced a 'benefits cap' in 2013. This placed a limit on the total amount of benefits that most people aged 16–64 can claim. It was designed to ensure that: households on out-of-work benefits would not get more in benefits than the average weekly wage; incentives to work would increase; greater fairness brought between those on out-of-work benefits and people in work; long-term dependency on benefits would reduce. In 2019, the cap was set at:

- £384.62 a week for couples (with or without children living with them) or single parents
- £257.69 a week for a single adult (no children or children don't live with them).

There have been some criticisms of the benefits cap. In 2018, the Work and Pensions Select Committee of the House of Commons reported that only 5% of those affected by the cap were moving from benefits to work and that 82% of those affected were in categories where they either could not work or were exempt from looking for work.

In 2017, Child Tax Credit or the 'child element' of Universal Credit was limited to two children only after this date as the government wanted to encourage families receiving benefits to think about the financial implications of having more than two children.

Welfare benefits in Scotland

The devolution of further powers to the Scottish Parliament by the Scotland Act (2016) included responsibility for 11 welfare benefits to be administered by Social Security Scotland, including:

Ill-health and disability benefits, such as Personal Independence Payments; Attendance Allowance and Severe Disablement Allowance; Carers Allowance

Best Start Grant (previously Sure Start Maternity Grant)

Cold Weather Payments and Winter Fuel Payments

Discretionary Housing Payments

The way in which some of these benefits are delivered is different than in the rest of the UK. For example, claimants can receive fortnightly instead of monthly payments to make it easier to manage their money and they can choose to have their housing benefit paid straight to their landlord to avoid building up rent arrears. In England and Wales, only one payment is made to an adult in a household where there might be more than one person in receipt of benefits, whereas in Scotland, payments are spilt to the adults within the household.

Means testing

Certain benefits are classed as **universal** – this means everyone is entitled to them no matter their financial situation. Until 2013, every family received child benefit; however, since then families where one parent earns more than £50,000 a year are unable to claim. This is what is referred to as means testing – claimants must declare the amount of income and capital they have, which then affects eligibility to claim. Means testing is regularly criticised on the basis that it is often complicated and costly to assess whether someone is entitled to benefits. Furthermore, it is argued that due to means testing a number of often needy recipients do not claim what they are entitled to, due to the complex nature of the application form or simply because they are unaware that they are entitled to further support. As a result, billions go unclaimed. In 2019, the charity Independent Age estimated that by 2022 the figure for unclaimed pension credit will have risen to £17 billion. Their campaign, 'Credit Where It's Due' is encouraging pensioners who qualify for the benefit to claim it; it's reckoned that if 75% of those eligible did sign up for it, half a million pensioners would be lifted out of poverty. The Department for Work and Pensions also estimated that 20% of families eligible for housing benefit and 16% of those eligible for income-related benefits did not claim. In its report, the DWP gave as reasons for this the 'attractiveness of the benefit, lack of awareness or the perceived stigma of receiving a benefit'.

> **TOP TIP**
>
> Use the UK government website to review further benefits available to UK citizens: https://www.gov.uk/browse/benefits

Quick Test

1. What should be the benefits of Universal Credit? List three criticisms of Universal Credit.
2. What did the introduction of the benefits cap mean for those claiming financial support?
3. Explain what you understand by the term 'means tested'.
4. What evidence is there that pensioner poverty could be reduced by a higher uptake of pension credit?
5. What reasons does the DWP give for some people not applying for benefits to which they may be entitled?

Attempts to reduce health inequalities

Smoking ban and the minimum unit pricing for alcohol

The ban on smoking in public places had a key aim: to reduce passive smoking. Scotland introduced the ban first, in March 2006, followed by Wales and Northern Ireland in April 2007, with England introducing the ban in July 2007.

A study of nine Scottish hospitals after the introduction of the smoking ban found that child asthma admissions had fallen by 18% and there had been a 17% reduction in heart attack admissions compared with a 5% per year increase before the ban. In May 2018, the Scottish Parliament set a minimum price on a unit of alcohol to try to reduce the harm caused by alcohol. People in Scotland drink 20% more alcohol than people in the rest of the UK. In June 2019, NHS Health Scotland reported that although Scots still drank more alcohol than the rest of the UK, they had bought less alcohol in 2018 than any year since the records began, and the gap between Scotland and the rest of the UK was narrowing.

Since March 2006, smoking has been banned in all enclosed public places in Scotland

Health promotion campaigns

This web page lists a range of policies and strategies implemented by both the UK and Scottish governments to promote an individual approach to a healthy lifestyle: https://patient.info/healthy-living/healthy-eating

The UK and Scottish governments have campaigns to encourage people to eat healthily

Eat Better Feel Better
This is a Scottish Government health promotion website that encourages healthy eating and a healthy lifestyle: www.eatbetterfeelbetter.co.uk

Change 4 Life
A UK government strategy to provide families with ideas, recipes and advice on how to live and eat well: www.nhs.uk/Change4Life/Pages/why-change-for-life.aspx

Active Schools
The Active Schools programme in Scotland employs specialist staff to provide more opportunities for children and young people to take part in sport and physical activity before school, during lunchtime and after school.

Screening programmes/HPV vaccine

Screening programmes and vaccinations are seen as a method of preventing future illness or identifying a killer disease early. Breast cancer is the most common cancer in Scottish women, accounting for 28.9% of female cancer cases. There are over 4,700 new cases of breast cancer diagnosed each year in women in Scotland. The Scottish Breast Screening Programme invites women aged between 50 and 70 for screening every three years. For women diagnosed with breast cancer, finding the disease early gives the best chance of successful treatment.

The human papillomavirus (HPV) vaccine for girls aged 11 to 13 years helps protect against cervical cancer. The HPV vaccine is offered to girls at secondary schools across Scotland.

In 2019, research published by Scottish universities showed that the high uptake of the HPV vaccine had led to 'a dramatic reduction in preinvasive cervical disease'.

Other screening programmes include those for heart disease, bowel cancer and cervical cancer.

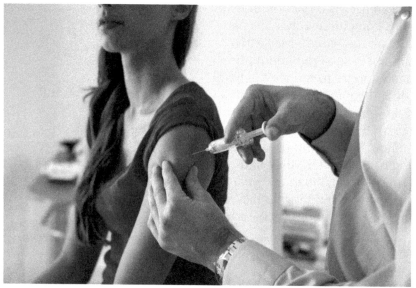

The human papillomavirus (HPV) vaccine helps protect against cervical cancer.

TOP TIP

For more information on Screening programmes, visit: https://www.gov.uk/topic/population-screening-programmes

Quick Test

1. What are two key benefits of screening programmes and vaccinations?
2. Have the smoking ban and minimum unit pricing of alcohol worked? Give evidence to support your answer.
3. In what ways might health promotion campaigns reduce levels of poor health?

Government legislation to reduce inequalities

The National Minimum Wage and the National Living Wage

The National Minimum Wage was introduced in 1999 by the Labour government in a bid to reduce poverty. Today, there are two types of minimum wage: The National Minimum Wage (NMW) and the National Living Wage (NLW). These are the legally-binding minimum hourly wages employers must pay. The NMW, which most workers aged 16–24 are entitled to varies by age from £3.90 for an apprentice to £7.70 for those aged 21–24. Workers over the age of 24 are paid the National Living Wage of £8.21 per hour. The government sets these rates each April in consultation with the Low Pay Commission. There is also a voluntary Real Living Wage (which should not be confused with these government schemes), which is recommended by the Living Wage Foundation, which argues that neither the NMW or the NLW are sufficient to meet people's needs. They recommend £9.00 across the UK and £10.55 in London. The government has set a target for the NLW reaching 60% of median earnings by 2020.

Equality Act (2010)

The Act legally protects people from discrimination in the workplace and wider society in an attempt to reduce inequalities. The Act replaced previous anti-discrimination laws with a single Act, making the law easier to understand and strengthening protection in some situations.

The Act states that it is unlawful to discriminate against anyone because of:

- Age
- Transgender
- Marriage/civil partnership
- Pregnancy
- Gender
- Ethnicity
- Sexual orientation
- Disability

It protects citizens in a number of situations including the workplace, education, using public services and buying or renting property.

Laws replaced by the Act include:

- Sex Discrimination Act (1975)
- Race Relations Act (1976)
- Disability Discrimination Act (1995)

GOT IT?

Maternity and paternity leave/pay

This ensures that employment rights are granted when on maternity leave, such as the right to pay rises, accruing holiday entitlement and the right to return to work. Legislation ensures that women are entitled to 52 weeks statutory maternity leave with statutory maternity pay being paid for 39 weeks.

Fathers are also guaranteed the opportunity to take paid leave on the birth of their children. Fathers are entitled to one or two weeks ordinary leave and up to 26 weeks paid additional paternity leave but only if the mother or co-adopter returns to work. If the parents of the child decide on Shared Parental Leave, this allows them to share up to 50 weeks of leave and 37 weeks of pay.

Fathers can also take paid leave when they have a baby

Quick Test

1. Explain the difference between the National Minimum Wage and the National Living Wage.
2. Why does the Living Wage Foundation recommend that employers pay the Real Living Wage?
3. Outline the key aims of the Equality Act (2010).
4. Explain how this Act has impacted on paternity leave/pay.

The role of the law in society

Rights and responsibilities

In the UK it is accepted that everyone is given legal rights, by law, and alongside these exist responsibilities; for example, we have the right to free speech when supporting a particular cause, however it is our responsibility not to make false or damaging statements against someone or an organisation. This would be regarded as slander, which is a criminal offence.

The law is therefore important in society in that it offers guidance and a set of norms with regard to behaviour. People will abide by the law as they are aware of the consequences of breaking the law. Without law, conflicts between individuals and groups would arise and it is argued society would be chaotic and anarchy would ensue. However, even with a robust system of law in place there is a constant need for the law to act, with the court system ruling on many different areas of criminal activity.

The role of the police

Police forces in the UK have a number of key functions:

- To maintain law and order.
- To protect members of the public and their property.
- To prevent crime.
- To reduce the fear of crime.
- To improve the quality of life of all citizens.

Police officers are also required to carry out certain tasks in relation to their work, such as attending community council meetings, submitting reports to the Procurator Fiscal's office in relation to criminal activity (Scotland), and they often have to attend court to give evidence.

Police officers carry out a variety of tasks

In 2012, the Scottish Government approved legislation to establish the Scottish Police Authority and Police Service of Scotland, known as 'Police Scotland', replacing the eight police forces that had existed formerly. The 17,000-strong force became the second largest force in the UK, after the Metropolitan Police in London. Iain Livingstone is the current Chief Constable of the unified force.

Post-Reform Policing Structure
Scottish Parliament
Scottish Ministers
Scottish Police Authority
Chief Constable
Local Commanders (×32)
Local Councils (×32)

The new policing structure

There were a number of reasons given for this reform including cost effectiveness, with a reported estimate of £47 million savings on officer costs within five years. However, critics saw the radical move as being driven purely by savings rather than by a desire to streamline the police force. Furthermore, critics viewed having only one Chief Constable as being susceptible to interference from the government, possibly leading to their having limited autonomy in decision making.

The Scottish Police Authority (SPA) was set up to hold the Chief Constable to account for the policing of Scotland. Chairman, businessman Vic Emery, said that the SPA would be a mechanism to 'scrutinise, test and approve' police decisions.

Although there is only one single force, it can be divided into three separate branches – uniform, criminal investigation (CID) and traffic. Specialised branches are also deployed at certain times; for example, dog, mounted, underwater and community.

TOP TIP

Read this article in the *Herald* to gain a broader understanding of the pros and cons of a single police force: www.heraldscotland.com/comment/herald-view/pros-and-cons-of-a-single-police-force.14716825

Quick Test

1. Outline the main roles of the police.
2. Explain, in detail, why the police force in Scotland was reformed to establish one force.
3. Why was the Scottish Police Authority set up?

Court structure

In the UK, the system of courts, known as the judiciary, interprets and applies the law in the name of the state. It is complicated in that the UK does not exist as a single body – Scotland and Northern Ireland operate under different legal arrangements than those in place in England and Wales. One feature that is common to all is the Supreme Court – the highest court of appeal. The law often appears further complicated as there are different legal pathways for different types of dispute.

The Supreme Court building entrance in London

Civil law

Civil law is concerned with the interrelationships and conflicts between different individuals and groups. Civil cases may involve matters such as disputes over wills or contracts. Cases brought to court under civil law are usually done so by individuals rather than the state and might often result in compensation being paid to the victim rather than a prison sentence.

Criminal law

Criminal law deals with crimes committed by an individual or group – violent behaviour, serious fraud, burglary, etc. Such cases are normally brought to court by the state and could lead to large fines or imprisonment.

TOP TIP

Research recent cases where the Supreme Court has heard appeals on behalf of Scottish prisoners. Can you think why the Scottish Government would be unhappy about this?

Court structure

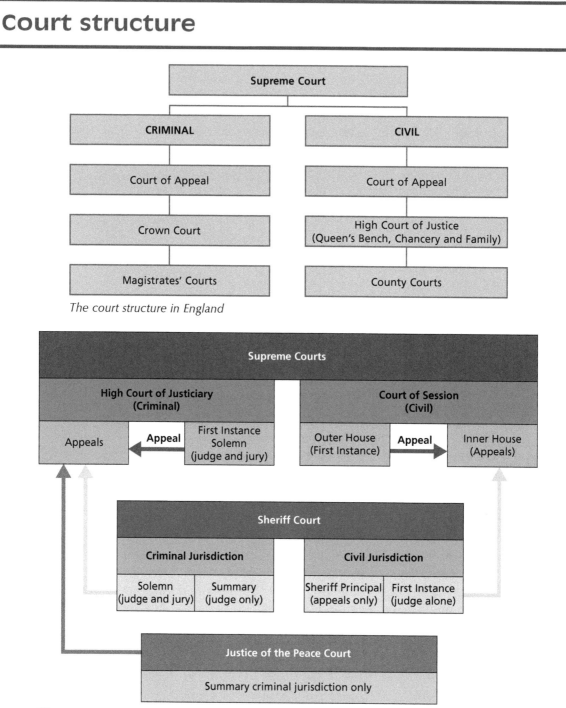

The court structure in England

The court structure in Scotland

Courts in Scotland have two different legal procedures: solemn and summary (see figure above). Solemn procedures involve the most serious criminal cases. These cases may lead to a trial, with a jury, in either the High Court or Sheriff Court. Summary cases, on the other hand, are less serious offences. Trials are conducted without a jury and may be heard in either the Sheriff Court or in a Justice of the Peace Court. One further difference that sets Scottish criminal courts apart is that they have three possible verdicts as opposed to two: guilty, not guilty and not proven.

The Scottish courts system

This table shows what each court can do in Scotland:

High Court of Justiciary	Highest criminal court in Scotland, dealing with the most serious of crimes: treason, murder and rape, armed robbery, drug trafficking and sexual offences involving children.	• Unlimited maximum fine • Unlimited maximum prison sentence
Sheriff Court	Deals with cases too serious for the Justice of the Peace courts but not serious enough for the High Court. Depending on evidence given in relation to a case, the Sheriff can refer a case to the High Court.	<u>Summary</u> • Maximum fine £5000 • Maximum prison sentence 12 months <u>Solemn</u> • Unlimited maximum fine • Maximum prison sentence five years (or pass to High Court) • Sheriffs can also issue alternatives to prison as well as more specific punishments, such as bans from social media such as Facebook and Twitter
Justice of the Peace Court	Lowest level of criminal court. Hears cases of breach of the peace, minor assaults, minor road traffic offences and petty theft.	• Maximum fine £2500 • Maximum prison sentence 60 days

Quick Test

1. Why do we regard the law as an important function of our society?
2. Explain why the UK court system is often referred to as 'complicated'.
3. Outline the difference between solemn and summary cases.

The penal system in Scotland

The Scottish Prison Service (SPS) is a Scottish government agency and was established in 1993.

The Scottish Prison Service

The purpose of the service is to maintain secure custody and good order within prisons, whilst caring for prisoners with humanity and delivering opportunities that give the best chance to reduce reoffending once a prisoner returns to the community. The SPS has 13 publicly managed prisons and two privately managed prisons.

It is widely acknowledged and accepted that certain individuals require a custodial sentence for a variable period of time, dependent on the crime for which they have been convicted. Supporters of prison would argue that it acts as a deterrent from committing crime or further crimes on release as well as a measure of ensuring public safety. Critics of prison, however, refer to the increasing cost of holding a prisoner for any length of time and the overcrowding within prisons. Furthermore, the high levels of reoffending suggest that prison does not always achieve its aims. Calls for alternatives to custodial sentences are often sought.

Alternatives to prison

Alternatives to custody are often referred to as **community sentencing**. Scotland is regarded as having one of the most extensive ranges of alternatives to custody in Europe. The most commonly used alternatives to custody are listed below.

Probation

Probation is the most frequently used community sentence. The main purpose of probation is to work with offenders to prevent or reduce their reoffending by providing opportunities for rehabilitation. Probation Orders can be used very flexibly by the courts and additional conditions can be attached to them; for example, requiring the offender to undertake unpaid work, or imposing an electronic tag.

Community Payback Orders

An offender given a community payback order is required to carry out unpaid work of benefit to the community for between 20 and 300 hours.

Restriction of Liberty Orders (tagging)

RLOs restrict offenders, who must be 16 or over, to a particular place or places for up to 12 hours per day for up to 12 months.

Drug Treatment and Testing Orders

DTTOs offer drug treatment and testing with regular reviews by the courts. These target people whose offending is linked to their drug problem; for example, those who steal to fund their drug habit. The intention of a DTTO is to help offenders overcome a drug addiction, thereby reducing or eliminating the need to reoffend.

Quick Test

1. List the key arguments for and against custodial sentences.
2. Outline the main alternatives to prison issued by Scottish courts.

Theories of crime

Individualist theories of crime

Individualist theories of crime relate generally to three key areas:
- Genetic theories
- Biological theories
- Psychological theories

Genetic theories

Cesare Lombroso (1876) identified that criminals had a number of similar characteristics:
- Large jaw
- High cheekbones
- Large ears
- Insensitivity to pain

However, Lombroso was heavily criticised because his research took place only in Italian prisons at a time when inmates were mainly poor and their physical appearance had been affected by the levels of deprivation from which they had suffered, alongside a poor diet. He was further criticised, as not everyone who commits a crime ends up in prison.

Sheldon & Eleanor Glueck, researchers working in the early to mid-1900s, identified relationships between physical build and 'delinquent' behaviour in males; delinquent referring here to deviant or criminal behaviour. Features of such 'delinquents' included a stocky, rounded build and being more active and aggressive. These researchers were criticised because what some people might see as 'active, aggressive delinquent' behaviour, others may not.

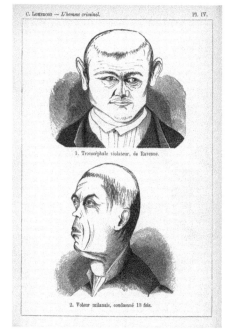

Illustrations from Lombroso's work

Y chromosome theory
Key features of this theory are:
- Extra Y chromosome.
- XYY chromosome makeup rather than XY.
- Studies in Denmark have indicated that men found with the extra Y chromosome were more frequently convicted of sexual abuse, arson and burglary.

The study acknowledged that the increase in crime rate may also have been related to deprivation and poor socio-economic conditions.

TOP TIP

Use www.sociology.org.uk to support your understanding of theories of crime.

Biological/psychological theories

Key features of these theories are:

- Crime is a form of illness.
- The criminal cannot help but commit crime.
- Result of a chemical imbalance in the brain.
- Born criminal.

Such theories are often based on the idea of **nature versus nurture**. Many murderers throughout history have had no real explanation for their criminal behaviour and theorists would argue they have an inherent impulse to kill. However, those who would support the **nurture** theory argue that criminals are not born this way; they are conditioned by society and environmental factors. There have been a number of studies carried out in an attempt to support such biological/psychological theories.

Adoption studies

Sarnoff A. Mednick analysed court convictions with 14,000 adoptees among them. Of these, he analysed the criminal records of both their adoptive parents and biological parents and found evidence to support the fact that those with biological parents who had criminal records were more likely to commit crime even when their adoptive parents had no criminal records. Further studies conducted in the US found that children born to incarcerated women, who were later adopted, were more likely to offend in later life. In Denmark, research highlighted a biological component for criminal acts against property – those whose biological fathers had been convicted of property crimes were more likely to engage in similar behaviour.

Further research would suggest that criminals often have specific personality traits or disorders. Eysenck highlighted that criminals often displayed 'extrovert' behaviour, that is, they acted impulsively, craved excitement and took risks. However, such theories have been criticised because people do not tend to behave in **one** particular way at all times. Some personality disorders originate in childhood. Attention deficit hyperactivity disorder (ADHD) and oppositional defiance disorder (ODD) are two common disorders that prisoners report having in their childhood, which have followed them into adulthood. Psychologists often argue that childhood experiences have a direct impact on criminal activity in later life.

Some research has found that children whose parents have criminal records are more likely to commit crime

Case study: Joanna Dennehy

Joanna Dennehy became the first woman in the UK to be sentenced to a full life term by a judge due to the nature of her crimes. One year prior to her committing these crimes she had been diagnosed with a personality disorder and was accused of lacking the normal range of human emotions.

Joanna Dennehy

Quick Test

1. What are the key features of a criminal as identified by Lombroso?
2. Outline the key features of the nature versus nurture debate?
3. Summarise the key arguments and criticisms of individualist theories of crime.

Social explanations of crime

Three key explanations of crime will be discussed here; however, you may have covered other theories in class.

Functionalist theory

Two key theories will be outlined under this heading – **strain theory** and **social control theory**.

Strain theory

According to strain theory, people become stressed or strained over a particular situation and as a result commit crime. It is argued that they engage in crime as a means to escape the particular stress or strain they are experiencing. A person may be stressed as a result of losing their job and being reliant on benefits and as a result steal to maintain the lifestyle to which they have become accustomed. On the other hand, it may be that the crime is in revenge for a previous crime that has caused stress or strain to that person or a family member. Agnew identifies two key types of strain:

In August 2014, Derek Grant admitted killing Patrick Bradley, who had stolen his son's iPhone

- Others preventing you from achieving your goals.
- Others taking things you value, which creates negative stimuli.

Strain theory can be related to the failure to achieve desired goals. Agnew links crime with failing to achieve desired goals: money and status for adults, and autonomy from adults for young people. The theory suggests that the further away you are from achieving the goal, the more likely that under strain you will commit a crime in order to move closer to the goal or desire.

Social control theory

Unlike strain theorists, who consider what pushes people into crime, control theorists look for reasons why most people conform in society. Control theorists such as Hirschi argue that there are three major types of social control that prevent people from committing crime:

- **Direct control** – family members, school teachers, work colleagues, the police.
- **Stake in conformity** – those with a lot to lose will fear being caught; this may be due to the emotional attachment to family or perhaps the attachment they have to society; people who have invested their time and effort in growing a business and developing a positive reputation are less likely to risk losing this through crime.
- **Internal control** – relates to the beliefs/values and self-control a person has; the more self-control an individual has, the less likely they are to engage in crime.

Social learning theory

Key features of this theory are:

- Crime occurs as a result of association with others – family/peer group.
- Learned behaviour – negative role models.
- Crime is viewed as desirable or justifiable in certain situations.
- The most obvious reason would be peer relations – a theory supported by the ever-growing number of gangs in the UK. However, crime can occur without any direct contact with others – evidence of growth in individual criminal activity is linked to engagement with particular films, mass media, computer games.

Extinction Rebellion protesters block city centre streets in Leeds

The Extinction Rebellion protests, such as the deliberate blocking of roads in cities such as Glasgow, London, Cardiff and Leeds in July 2019 to draw attention to climate change, were viewed by many as a justifiable breaking of the law.

Interactionist theory – labelling theory

Theorists would argue that continued crime can be a consequence of official efforts to control crime. Once a criminal has been arrested, prosecuted and punished they have been labelled a criminal. This then reinforces the fact that they have a different position in society to others and often prevents them from moving away from criminal activity. A criminal record may prevent someone from getting a particular job and in order to survive, that person may continue to engage in crime, as they perceive themselves to be worth nothing better. John Braithwaite argued that although this could be true for some, it might not be the case for all. He argued that in some situations crime would decrease as a result of reintegration into society – the criminal who feels ashamed or guilty for their actions, or the criminal who has been forgiven by his or her family or peer group, may not feel the need or urge to engage in further criminal activity.

> **TOP TIP**
>
> Do some research: use online newspapers to find criminal activity that could be argued to have occurred as a result of **labelling**.

Quick Test

1. What are the two key theories that come under the heading of functionalist theory?
2. Outline the three measures of social control offered by Hirschi.
3. Summarise the key features of social learning theory.

The impact of crime on society: economic

Crime not only leads to numerous financial and emotional costs for those who have been victims, but crime also forces local and national governments to spend billions on the prevention of crime and the detection, prosecution and punishment of criminals. We can therefore argue that there are economic consequences of crime for the individual, the taxpayer and the government.

The rising costs of crime

Violent crime costs the UK £50 billion a year.

Recent report from the Home Office shows that crimes against the person are costing the country over £50 billion every year with 115 retail workers attacked every day.

The rising costs of crime

In the 2018 Home Office report, 'The Economic and Social Costs of Crime' it was estimated that, for England and Wales, the total cost of crimes against the individual was £50 billion. Each homicide was reckoned to cost £3,217,740 and the total cost of crimes involving violence with injury was put at £15.5 billion. These figures were calculated by taking into account the costs in anticipation of the crime (e.g. fitting burglar alarms), the consequences of the crime (e.g. medical treatment of injuries) and costs in response to crime (costs to the police and criminal justice system). In 2019, the Retail Crime Survey put the total cost of crime to the retail sector at £1.9 billion per annum with 115 employees being attacked each day at their place of work.

TOP TIP

For further information on the impact of crime in England and Wales, go to https://www.gov.uk/government/publications/the-economic-and-social-costs-of-crime

The impact of serious organised crime

According to the National Crime Agency (NCA), serious and organised crime is costing the UK economy £37 billion each year. The agency estimates that there are over 4,500 serious organised crime groups (SOCGs) in the UK and that their impact on the people of the UK is greater than all other security threats put together. Lynne Owens, the Director General of the NCA has stated, 'Each year it kills more of our citizens than terrorism, war and natural disasters combined'. The cost of SOCG activity has risen sharply since the last estimate in 2013, which put the figure at £24 billion. Such criminal groups will often be involved in a wide range of activities including drug and people trafficking, counterfeiting, cyber crime, fraud and money laundering. The profits, according to Police Scotland, 'are invested in other types of criminal activity, thus fuelling a "cycle of crime"'. The impact on communities can be seen in a 2018 study, 'Community experiences of serious organised crime in Scotland' commissioned by the Scottish Government in which it was shown that, although SOCGs often operated across a wide geographical area, they tended to impact more in the lives of people living in the more deprived areas of the country in which 'organised' crime frequently featured as a relatively routine aspect of everyday life.

Serious organised crime kills more people than terrorism, war and natural disasters combined

Quick Test

1. What does crime force local and national governments to do that leads to growing financial burden?
2. What factors are taken into account when calculating the cost of a crime?
3. Describe the impacts that serious organised crime has on both local communities and the country.

The impact of crime on society: social

Crime not only has economic consequences but communities are often labelled as dangerous and recognised for their high crime rate as opposed to positive factors. As a result, crime in these communities often becomes commonplace and so they continue to suffer the consequences of crime. The negative impact continues further as fear in these communities gradually rises, with residents becoming 'withdrawn, defenseless and less committed to their communities' (source: http://law.jrank.org/pages/12125/Economic-Social-Effects-Crime.html). The value of housing decreases, with fewer businesses willing to invest in the area. Public opinion would often suggest that these types of communities are areas with high levels of deprivation; however, there are a number of more affluent areas where crime rates are significant.

Poverty and crime: Case study: Glasgow

Although there is a clear link between poverty and higher levels of crime, it is wrong to suggest that poverty alone is the cause of crime. The vast majority of people living in poorer areas are law abiding. In fact, people living in poor areas are much more likely to be the victims of crime than those living in more affluent areas. For many years, Glasgow has been the poorest area in Scotland with child poverty levels of 34% according to the Glasgow Centre for Population Health, while the more affluent area of East

Glasgow experiences higher levels of crime than more affluent areas

Renfrewshire has child poverty levels of 16%. Scottish Government analyses of crime in these two areas show that Glasgow experienced 708 crimes per 1000 people in 2017–18 whereas East Renfrewshire experienced 263 per 1000 people. People living in poorer areas are much more likely to live near criminals and be their victims. For example they are much more likely to be:

- assaulted
- robbed and mugged
- burgled
- sexually assaulted
- victims of domestic violence

Further impact
- Lack of facilities in the area.
- A reduction in potential job opportunities.
- Social exclusion – crime culture accepted.
- Poor reputation.

The impact of 'white collar crime'

While much of the crime experienced in Glasgow might be called 'blue collar' crime – i.e. committed by people from a working-class background where the damage done to the victim, property or area is obvious, so-called middle-class or 'white collar' crime also affects society. This type of crime includes activities such as fraud, bribery, embezzlement, cyber crime, identity theft and tax evasion. A recent National Audit Office Report estimated that white collar crime cost businesses in the UK £144bn and individuals £10bn and HMRC £10bn per annum. This means that businesses have to pass the cost on to customers, individuals lose savings and the government has less money to spend on public services such as schools and hospitals.

Impact of crime on the victim

Crime affects people in many different ways, whether it be in the short- or long-term. Victim Support reports that how people react to crimes will depend on each individual and on the following factors:

- The type of crime.
- Whether the victim knows the person who committed the crime.
- The support that the victim gets (or doesn't get) from family, friends, the police and others.
- Things that have happened in the past (because if the victim has had to deal with difficult events before, they may have found ways of coping).

Victim Support state that certain emotions such as anger or fear are common after being the victim of a crime; however, some victims appear to suffer no immediate impact, feeling 'normal' for a while and then experiencing some form of anxiety at a later date. As a result of the anxiety or fear, perhaps having been the victim of an unprovoked attack or more seriously a sexual assault, victims can sometimes suffer physical symptoms such as lack of sleep, depression or, at the most extreme, feeling compelled to take their own lives because they are unable to cope with the pressures and mental strain of what has happened to them. This may be true of victims who feel vulnerable or powerless, especially where the crime is on-going; for example, in cases of domestic abuse or racial violence. In 2017, Justene Reece took her own life after being subjected to six months of stalking and harassment by her ex-partner. Although she had reported the threats to the police on 34 occasions, they had failed to record them properly, which meant that officers did not have a proper idea of the extent of the threat. She killed herself in February 2017 leaving a note saying she had 'run out of fight' after six months of threats of violence.

TOP TIP

To learn more about the impact of crime on the individual, visit the website of Victim Support: https://www.victimsupport.org.uk/help-and-support/coping-crime/how-can-crime-affect-you

PC David Rathband

Victims of crime may also suffer varying levels of economic impact. Should the victim have suffered extreme physical injury they may not be able to return to their previous occupation. In the case of PC David Rathband (above), being shot and blinded by Raoul Moat in 2010 had the most serious impact possible. PC Rathband was unable to return to his traffic police job as a result of his injuries and struggled to cope with his immediate and irreparable disabilities – 20 months after the attack, he killed himself.

Quick Test

1. What factors affect how individuals react to being victims of crime?
2. What evidence is there that crime and poverty may be linked?
3. Explain the difference between 'blue collar' and 'white collar' crime?

The impact of crime on the offender

Crime and the offender

The impact of crime on the offender varies, again generally depending on the crime committed. For instance, the impact of using illegal drugs on a recreational basis could lead to a criminal record as well as the potential development of a drug habit, with many drug addicts resorting to further crimes, such as shoplifting, to fund their addiction. Criminals in these situations will often find it hard, if not impossible, to hold down a job; the further consequence of a criminal record being the impact it has on future employment. Furthermore, whilst taking drugs many addicts find a major deterioration in their physical and mental health, with some facing the most extreme situations; for example, contracting HIV through the sharing of needles or death as a result of an overdose.

The CRB holds records of criminal activity

Alongside this, the majority of employers will ask about previous convictions and 4 million Criminal Records Bureau (CRB) checks are carried out every year in England and Wales. There are a growing number of professions where criminal records are never lifted, such as doctors, nurses, teachers, police officers and lawyers. Anyone applying to study specific courses in the health, social care and education fields will be subject to scrutiny. If found to have a criminal conviction, it is likely that their application will be refused, leading to limited opportunities for educational progression.

Criminal convictions may also impact on the ability to travel – difficulties will be encountered when applying for visas to enter certain countries. In order to gain entry into the USA, for instance, the visitor must declare all convictions and each case is dealt with on an individual basis.

Convicted criminals may also suffer in relation to housing. Criminals who are given a prison sentence may ultimately have to give up their property and may end up homeless on release due to some prisoners finding that family relationships break down as a result of a prison sentence. Furthermore, when applying for a mortgage, convictions must be declared – this may have an impact on your suitability for a loan.

Finally, it is evident that there can be psychological implications to having a criminal record – notably shame and embarrassment.

Quick Test

1. Describe how the taking of drugs recreationally can lead to a far greater negative impact on the offender than crime alone.
2. Which professions are you prevented from working in if you have a criminal conviction?
3. List three ways that life may be affected as a result of having a criminal record.

Measures to tackle crime and their effectiveness

'My job is to make your streets safer. We need to come down hard on crime. That means coming down hard on criminals'

Prime Minister Boris Johnson, August 2019

Tackling crime in England and Wales

Figures published by the Office for National Statistics in 2019 show that for England and Wales, the overall level of crime, after falling for several years, remained 'relatively stable', but within this overall measure of total crime there were increases and decreases in certain types of crime. Crimes involving theft and fraud, for example, had increased as had 'higher-harm' types of violence including stabbings, while there was a 4% reduction in homicides after several years of increase. The long-term trends show that crime has been decreasing for the last 20 years but this decrease has slowed

Crime prevention measures reduce crime rates across local communities

down most recently. Evidence of this falling trend in violence was provided by the Violence Research Group and the Cardiff University annual survey in 2018 which showed that violence-related admissions to hospitals were 41% lower than in 2010.

In the UK it is the responsibility of the Home Office to prevent crime in England and Wales and to ensure that measures are effectively taken to reduce crime rates across local communities.

In 2016, the then Home Secretary Theresa May introduced 'The Modern Crime Prevention Strategy'. This strategy was aimed at preventing crime by focusing on what it called the six key drivers of crime: opportunity, character, the effectiveness of the Criminal Justice System, profit, drugs and alcohol. Each of these drivers would be tackled to reduce the likelihood of crime:

- Opportunity: removing or 'designing out' opportunities to offend, offline and online.
- Character: early intervention with those who are more likely to offend.
- Effectiveness of the Criminal Justice System: to ensure effective deterrence.
- Profit: making it harder for criminal to profit from crime.
- Drugs: disrupt the supply, help people to avoid drugs and help people to stop using them.
- Alcohol: prevent alcohol-related crime and disorder.

When Boris Johnson became Prime Minister in July of 2019, his focus was on 'coming down hard on criminals'. To this end, he announced a number of measures including 20,000 more police officers, 10,000 more prison places, improved prison security, and greater use of 'stop and search'.

Tackling crime in Scotland

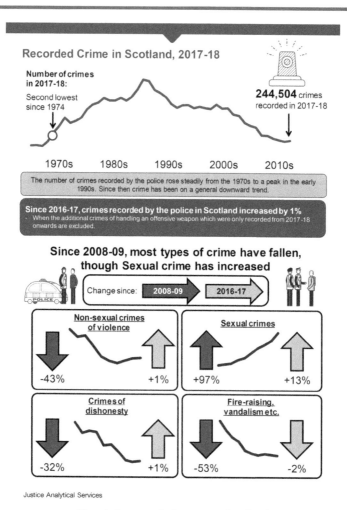

Trends in recorded crime in Scotland

The Scottish Government set out its crime prevention policy in the document 'Justice in Scotland: Vision and Priorities 2017 to 2020' in which it identified a range of crimes it was focusing on, including:

- human trafficking
- serious organised crime
- violence against women and girls
- violence and knife crime
- hate crime
- the sharing of intimate images or video without consent
- cyber crime
- sexual offences committed against children
- introducing drug driving limits and roadside testing in October 2019

Strategies to tackle these crimes included investing in policing and addressing 'the root causes of crime, including poverty and inequality, adverse childhood experiences and drugs and alcohol'.

Equally Safe: Scotland's strategy to eradicate violence against women

TOP TIP

For further information on crime levels and measures to tackle crime, use the following links:

- Scottish Crime and Justice Survey 2017–18: https://gov.scot/publications/scottish-crime-justice-survey-2017-18-main-findings/

- Equally Safe strategy: https://www.gov.scot/policies/violence-against-women-and-girls/equally-safe-strategy/

- Justice in Scotland: Vision and Priorities: https://www.gov.scot/publications/justice-scotland-vision-priorities/

Quick Test

1. Explain what is meant by 'drivers of crime'.

2. In what ways does Prime Minister Johnson intend to 'come down hard on crime'?

3. What, according to the Scottish Government, are some of the 'root causes of crime'?

Tackling crime case studies

Tackling hate crime

In October 2018, the Home Office published a Statistical Bulletin on hate crime in England and Wales. In that bulletin it was recorded that there were 94,098 hate crime offences recorded by the police in England and Wales in 2017/18, which represented an increase of 17% on the previous year. This continued what the bulletin called 'the upward trend in recent years'. In fact, since 2012/13 there had been a 123% increase in hate crimes recorded by the police. This increase was attributed to several factors including better police recording of hate crimes and reactions to events including the EU referendum and terrorism attacks such as the Westminster Bridge attack.

Hate graffiti

The following number of hate crimes were reported in 2017/18:

- 71,251 (76%) race hate crimes
- 11,638 (12%) sexual orientation hate crimes
- 8,336 (9%) religious hate crimes
- 7,226 (8%) disability hate crimes
- 1,651 (2%) transgender hate crimes

In 2016, the Conservative government introduced its policy 'Action Against Hate' focused on five themes: preventing hate crime by challenging beliefs and attitudes; responding to hate crime within our communities; increasing the reporting of hate crime; improving support for victims of hate crime; and building our understanding of hate crime. Alongside this Action Plan, the government introduced its 'Integrated Communities Plan' in 2019, which aimed to promote better integration amongst communities by such things as creating opportunities for people to mix with those from other backgrounds, boosting English language skills, and supporting migrants to develop a good understanding of life in England.

Reducing knife, gun and gang crime

Although overall crime has fallen consistently until fairly recently, Home Office figures for knife crime for 2019 showed an 80% increase from 2014. A total of 43 out of 44 police authorities reported rising levels of knife crime since 2011, with victims getting younger and wounds more severe. In April 2018, the government introduced its 'Serious Violence Strategy'. Aims included tackling so-called county lines gangs from the cities who target smaller towns and often use children as drug couriers; early intervention and prevention; and supporting communities to prevent potential violence.

In July 2019, the Home Secretary announced a further series of measures to support this strategy:

All public bodies, including the police, councils, local health bodies, youth offending services and schools now had a 'health duty' to work together to prevent and tackle serious violence.

The Crime and Disorder Act was amended to make violence prevention a compulsory top priority for Community Safety Partnerships.

An Early Intervention Youth Fund of £22m was distributed among 'target' areas to support projects to divert young people away from crime.

Further money was also put into the Anti-Knife Crime Community Fund.

Drawing on the example of the Scottish Violence Reduction Unit (see below) the Home Secretary allocated £35m to the police in 18 areas to set up Violence Reduction Units. In May 2019, the Offensive Weapons Act strengthened police response to violent crime and the use of knifes and other weapons such as acid.

The Scottish Violence Reduction Unit (SVRU)

In 2005, when the Scottish Violence Reduction Unit (SVRU) was established, Scotland was labeled as 'Europe's murder capital'. The SVRU took a 'public health approach' to violence, regarding it is a 'sickness' that could be cured by tackling its root causes, working alongside other agencies such as the police, hospitals and schools to engage with young people and to divert them from violence. In 2004/5 there were 137 homicides in Scotland. By 2018 this had fallen to 59. Deputy Director Will Linden, when asked about how London should tackle violence, summed up the approach of the SVRU: 'We know that working together communities, police and services can and do save lives. Violence isn't inevitable and can be prevented.'

> **TOP TIP**
>
> Government strategies to reduce terror-related crimes are covered in Unit 3.

Quick Test

1. What evidence is there that the government's measures to tackle hate crime are not effective?

2. Outline the measures taken by the government recently to tackle the issues related to hate crime.

3. What evidence is there that the approach taken by the Scottish Violence Reduction Unit is effective?

Alcohol

Alcohol-related crime

Although drinkers in the UK consume only slightly over the average alcohol per person, in the European Union, according to the charity Alcohol Aware, the UK 'is consistently among the highest for binge drinking…'. On average, drinking in the UK tends to involve more drunkenness than elsewhere. Figures compiled by Alcohol Aware for England and Wales in 2017/18 showed that:

- Alcohol-related violent incidents made up 67% of violent incidents that take place at the weekend.

- 12.4% of theft offences, 20.6% of criminal damage and 21.5% of hate crimes were alcohol-related.

- In 35.8% of sexual assault cases, the offender was under the influence of alcohol.

- Over 9,000 people were killed or injured in drink driving incidents in 2016.

The issue of alcohol-related crime was recognised in the Modern Crime Prevention Strategy (see above) as one of the key drivers of crime. Measures to reduce and prevent alcohol related crime in England and Wales include:

Local Alcohol Action Areas were set up to 'tackle the harmful effects of irresponsible drinking, particularly alcohol-related crime and disorder'. Local licensing authorities, health bodies and the police work together to reduce alcohol-related crime.

The Troubled Families programme – to support at-risk families, including those with alcohol-related issues.

Courts can issue Alcohol Treatment Requirement (ATR) orders to people who have committed offences related to alcohol.

Alcohol and crime in Scotland

'There is a strong link between alcohol and violent crime.' This statement was made by Alcohol Focus Scotland (AFS) in its 2018 report 'Alcohol and Violent Crime'. Although the amount of alcohol per head consumed in Scotland is reducing, it is still higher than any other part of the UK. In its 2018 report, AFS stated that 42% of violent crime in Scotland is alcohol-related and that almost 100,000 alcohol-related violent crimes still take place in Scotland each year.

Measures introduced in a bid to control the problem are detailed below.

Alcohol (Minimum Pricing) (Scotland) Act 2012

This act came into effect on 1 May 2018 (it took six years to come into force due to court objections by the alcohol industry). A minimum price for alcohol sets the lowest price an alcoholic drink can be sold for. In Scotland, the minimum price per unit of alcohol was set at 50p. Although it is difficult to measure the impact of the Act as it has only been in force for a short time, NHS Scotland reported that in 2018, Scots had bought less alcohol than any year since records began in the 1990s. Before the Act was introduced, research from the University of Sheffield found that a proposed minimum price of 50p per unit would result in the following benefits:

The legal alcohol limit has been reduced

- A fall in crime volumes by around 3500 offences per year.
- A financial saving from harm reduction (health, employment, crime etc.) of £942m over 10 years.

Drink driving limit

In 2014, the Scottish Parliament voted unanimously in favour of a law reducing the legal alcohol limit from 80 mg to 50 mg in every 100 ml of blood. The introduction of the new law brought Scotland in line with most other European countries; however, it does make the law different from that in England and Wales. Campaigners for the change suggested that it would cut the number of deaths and serious injuries on the road. The UK government, however, have no plans to reduce the drink driving limit elsewhere in the UK, with the view that it will have no real effect on 'serious offenders'. In 2018, the Glasgow University Institute of Health and Wellbeing issued a report showing that the new lower level had not had the impact hoped for in reducing road traffic accidents. Professor Jim Lewsey said that this 'surprising' finding was probably because the policy 'was not backed up with sufficient police enforcement or media campaigning'.

Quick Test

1. List three pieces of evidence to show the link between alcohol and criminal behaviour.
2. Outline how the two measures introduced in Scotland aim to tackle alcohol-related crime.
3. How effective have these measures been?

USA

Background information

Is the USA powerful? Let us look at the facts and figures:

- 9,826,630 square kilometres.
- Approximately half the land area of Russia.
- Slightly larger in area than China.
- UK could fit into the state of Texas alone.
- Population – 319,643,320 as at September 2019.
- Large variety of water, mineral, agricultural resources.
- Basis for highly productive economy.
- World's wealthiest nation by GDP.
- Leading country in world affairs.
- Influential member of international organisations such as UN and World Bank.
- Leader in a number of defence organisations such as NATO.
- Large number of nuclear weapons.
- Perhaps the most powerful military in the world.

The American people

The US population is made up of five main ethnic groups:

- White
- Hispanic
- African American
- Asian and Pacific Islanders (APIs are sometimes discussed as two separate ethnic groups)
- Native American

TOP TIP

Use www.census.gov for quick, easy to access facts about the people, business and geography of the USA.

Quick Test

1. To develop your knowledge of each of the ethnic groups, create a fact file for each group. Include:

   - % of total population
   - Sub groups
   - Settlement patterns
   - Explanation of settlement pattern
   - Key issues facing each group

The political system of the USA

Constitutional arrangements

When the Founding Fathers were writing the constitution, they included a whole range of compromises. These ensured that no one person or small group of people would have complete control of government and decision making in the USA. The codified constitution therefore established a full and authoritative set of rules written down in a single text.

What did it establish?

Article I: established **Congress** as the national legislature that would be made up of two chambers, laid down the methods of election, terms of office and powers.

Article II: established a **President** of the USA, laid down methods of election, terms of office and powers.

Article III: established the **US Supreme Court**, laid down the judges' terms of office and their jurisdiction.

Bill of Rights

Attached to the first seven articles were 10 amendments known as the **Bill of Rights**. These were designed to protect American citizens from an over-powerful federal government.

TOP TIP

Use this link to gain further information on the Bill of Rights and what it means for US citizens: http://cdn4. kidsdiscover.com/wp-content/ uploads/2012/09/Bill-of-Rights-Kids-Discover.jpg

Separation of powers

The Constitution further guaranteed certain fundamental constitutional rights by separating the power of government into three different 'branches'. The government – federal, state or local – must take steps to ensure that these rights are effectively protected. All three branches of the federal government play an important role.

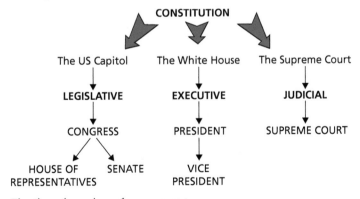

The three branches of government

- Legislative Branch (makes the laws).
- Executive Branch (carries out the laws).
- Judicial Branch (enforces the law and interprets the law).

The Founding Fathers also had the idea that each of these three independent yet equal branches should check the power of the other.

Checks and balances

SYSTEM OF CHECKS AND BALANCES IN THE US FEDERAL GOVERNMENT

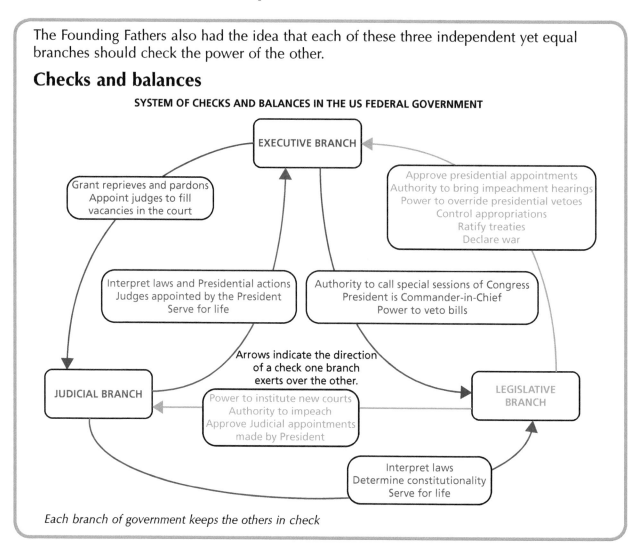

Each branch of government keeps the others in check

Rights and responsibilities of US citizens

The first amendments to the Constitution, known as the Bill of Rights, aimed to protect the citizens of the US. The US Citizenship and Immigration Service continues to highlight that all US citizens should be able to exercise and respect certain rights and responsibilities.

Rights
✓ Freedom to express yourself.
✓ Freedom to worship as you wish.
✓ Right to a prompt, fair trial by jury.
✓ Right to vote in elections for public officials.
✓ Right to run for elected office.
✓ Freedom to enjoy 'life, liberty, and the pursuit of happiness'.

Responsibilities
✓ Support and defend the Constitution.
✓ Participate in the democratic process.
✓ Respect and obey federal, state and local laws.
✓ Respect the rights, beliefs and opinions of others.
✓ Serve on a jury when called upon to do so.
✓ Defend the country if the need should arise.

Every US citizen has certain rights and responsibilities

However, due to differing state laws with regard to controversial topics such as gun control, capital punishment and same-sex marriage, some US citizens believe their rights are being breached.

Case study: 'Human Life Protection Act' – Alabama

In May 2019, the state legislature in Alabama passed the controversial Human Life Protection Act, which has been described as a 'near total ban' on termination of pregnancy, including in cases of rape and incest. Under this act, doctors who attempted to terminate a pregnancy faced a 10-year prison sentence and a 99-year sentence for carrying out the procedure. The only exception to this law is if the mother's life is at serious risk. Opponents of the law such as The National Organization for Women called the ban 'unconstitutional', while pro-life supporters of the Act argue that all human life should be protected.

Quick Test

1. Using the two diagrams, explain in detail what is meant by the terms 'separation of powers' and 'checks and balances'.
2. Provide evidence (actual examples) of the checks each branch provides on the others.
3. Why do some US citizens believe their rights are being breached?

The powers of the President

The President of the USA

The President of the USA is perhaps the world's best-known public figure and is often referred to as the most powerful person in the world. The powers of the President are set out in Article II of the Constitution and provide him with significant power to govern. However, the Constitution, as stated previously, ensures that there are 'checks and balances' on this power.

In January 2017, real estate mogul and TV reality star, Donald Trump was inaugurated as the 45th President of the USA, defeating the Democratic candidate, Hilary Clinton.

Donald Trump, 45th President

Head of State

As Head of State, the President represents the nation at home and abroad. He has the power and authority to receive other foreign heads of state and offers diplomatic recognition in the exchange of foreign ambassadors. However, these duties as Head of State are more ceremonial and are often not seen as conveying any real or meaningful power.

Patronage

The power of patronage allows the President to appoint secretaries of state to run government departments. In July 2019, Trump appointed Mark Esper as the next Secretary of Defense. Presidential power is 'checked' on these occasions by the Senate. The Senate hold nomination hearings and debate the benefits and consequences of such appointments before voting on the final outcome. The President also has the power to appoint all federal judges to fill vacancies caused by death or retirement.

Legislative function

The President has the power to recommend legislation to Congress – he does this in January of each year at the State of the Union address. One of President Trump's most high-profile policies, and a major campaign promise is to 'build a wall' on the USA–Mexico border to stop people crossing into the USA 'illegally'. The funding of this must be approved by Congress. On several occasions this funding has been either reduced or rejected by the Democrat-controlled House of Representatives, which has also tried to restrict the President's power to wage war by stopping the President from attacking Iran without first getting the approval of Congress.

Veto

The President has the power to veto bills passed by Congress. He returns the bill to Congress, unsigned, with an explanation of why he has exercised his power. Congress has the choice to either amend the legislation or attempt to overturn the veto. In order to overturn the veto, Congress needs to gain a two-thirds majority in both the Senate and the House of Representatives. Since coming to power, President Trump has used his veto five times up to September 2019. In July 2019, he vetoed attempts by Congress to block multibillion dollar arms sales by the USA to Saudi Arabia and the United Arab Emirates.

Executive order

The President can bypass Congress and issue regulations under an executive order. A President would use this in times of emergency or for a particular situation. An executive order has the binding force of the law and requires no congressional approval. Since coming to power, President Trump has issued 122 executive orders in the less than three years he has been president. This compares with 291 by George Bush and 276 by Barak Obama over their 8-year terms of office. After failing in an attempt to have a question about US citizenship included in the 2020 census, President Trump issued an Executive Order requiring the Department of Commerce to obtain citizenship data through other government agencies, including Homeland Security and Social Security.

National security

The President is the Commander-in-Chief of the Armed Forces and is charged with the defence of the USA. He can order the use of troops overseas without declaring war; however, he needs congressional approval to officially declare war on a country.

> **TOP TIP**
>
> Use your research skills to gather information on the most recent occasions that the President has exercised his powers and how this power has been checked – it is best practice to have the most up-to-date information.

Quick Test

1. What are the key powers of the US President?
2. How does the President use his position and power to influence the US Congress and the Supreme Court?

Influencing the political system

Opportunities for participation

There are various ways that ordinary Americans can participate in the political system of the USA.

Voting booth

- **Voting** – at federal, state and local levels, there are regular opportunities to take part in democratic elections. Approximately 450,000 elections are held in the USA each year. Many elections, such as those for state governor or major city mayors, attract significant media attention. However, those for school boards and city councils have a low profile.

- **Standing as a candidate** – US citizens may choose to run as a candidate for a number of positions, including congressman or woman, or state governor.

- **Supporting a candidate** – party members can get involved in the political campaign, of a candidate by delivering leaflets, displaying posters or canvassing through a 'phonebank'. Candidates rely on this support for success.

- **Contributing to party funds/campaign** – during the 2020 presidential campaign, high-profile celebrities, as well as ordinary citizens, made huge contributions to both Democrats and Republicans. In the run-up to the 2020 Presidential election, the Democrats were given public support by 'stars' such as Beyonce, Robert De Niro and Tom Hanks; while President Trump was backed by Kelsey Grammar, Clint Eastwood and Kanye West among others, with many of these celebrities contributing to campaign funds.

- **Joining an interest group** – interest groups attempt to put pressure on the government and influence the amendments or introduction of laws. Interest groups will use methods such as marches, demonstrations and petitions to attract support for their cause. They may also lobby congressmen and women or use the media to publicise their campaign for political change. High-profile interest groups in the USA gain huge amounts of publicity and are often perceived to be highly influential. Examples include: The National Rifle Association (NRA), the Coalition to Stop Gun Violence (CSGV) and The American Association of Retired Persons (AARP).

TOP TIP

Ensure that you have a sound knowledge of a current interest group in the USA. The following link will be useful: https://votesmart.org/interest-groups#.XYHy-ChKg2x. You should aim to find out who they are, what their main cause for concern is, how they have attempted to gain publicity and whether or not they have been influential.

Fair and equal participation?

Participation in the USA is not always consistent and therefore neither is the political influence of American citizens. Before voting, citizens must register to vote. This appears to be the first issue regarding influence.

According to the Organisation for Economic Cooperation and Development (OECD), in 2018, the USA was ranked 26th out of 32 member states for voter turnout. In the 2016 presidential elections only 55% of registered voters actually voted, with Black and Hispanic groups having lower turnout rates than Whites. This is often attributed to the fact that the registration procedure can be complicated and some groups don't value voting and so don't see the point in registering. As a result, turnout is never as high as it could be. Some Americans don't vote due to 'voting fatigue' – a high number of official posts are elected and people are put off by elections occurring so often. Certain Americans, such as Blacks and Hispanics, do not feel voting will change their lives or improve their situation so they do not value the electoral process. Furthermore, many Hispanics are illegal immigrants and are therefore not eligible to vote (the most recent Pew Research suggests that there are approximately 11.1 million illegal immigrants in the USA, over 80% of whom are Hispanic/Latino – approximately 9 million).

Influence of ethnic minorities

In the 2016 Presidential election there were significant differences in the way ethnic groups voted for the Democrat candidate Hilary Clinton and the Republican candidate Donald Trump. Of the Whites who voted, 57% voted for Trump while 89% of African Americans voted for Clinton. The Hispanic vote showed a similar pattern of favouring Clinton with 66% voting for her and only 28% voting for Trump. This pattern was repeated in the 2018 mid-terms with 90% of Blacks and 69% of Hispanics voting for Democratic candidates and 54% of Whites voting Republican.

Ethnic minorities in 114th Congress

Following the 2018 midterm elections, the racial diversity of Congress increased for the fifth time in a row with 22% of members from a racial or ethnic minority. However, although ethnic minorities make up 22% of Congress, they actually make up 39.2% of the total US population.

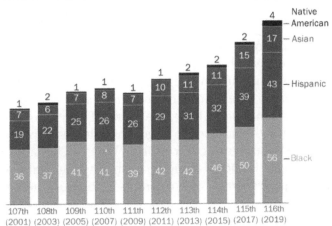

Growing racial and ethnic diversity in Congress

Number of nonwhite U.S. House and Senate members by race/ethnicity

Native American, Asian, Hispanic, Black

107th (2001), 108th (2003), 109th (2005), 110th (2007), 111th (2009), 112th (2011), 113th (2013), 114th (2015), 115th (2017), 116th (2019)

Note: Nonvoting delegates and commissioners excluded. Figures represent makeup of Congress on the first day of each session. Only first year of each Congress is labeled. Asian includes Pacific Islanders. Members who have more than one racial or ethnic identity are counted in each applicable group.
Source: Congressional Research Service, CQ Roll Call, Brookings Institution.

PEW RESEARCH CENTER

How influential are minority groups overall?

It may be that minority groups have more influence than you would first think. In Congress, the minority vote can be influential – in the House of Representatives, 218 votes are required to pass a bill. Minorities, if they make a united stand, can provide more than half of the vote required.

In a bid to attract the Hispanic vote, the Trump 2020 campaign set up 'Latinos for Trump'

Ethnic minorities overwhelmingly vote Democrat as a result of their policies and strategies, which have been devised to support ethnic minorities and the issues they face (poverty, poor healthcare, etc.). In turn, White candidates/congressmen and women may well support these policies given that they will rely on the votes of minorities in their congressional districts or local areas. Furthermore, it is evident that the support is valued, looking at the number of ongoing strategies adopted to encourage ethnic minorities to register and turn out to vote – 'Vote or Die' and 'Declare Yourself' were prominent campaigns in the past and Spanish-language campaign materials as well as Spanish-language registration forms are used to court the Hispanic vote.

Quick Test

1. Explain why it is reasonable to suggest that American citizens have a number of opportunities to participate in politics.

2. What evidence is there to suggest that Americans do not participate in politics as fully as they could?

3. Outline three pieces of evidence that would suggest ethnic minorities are actually more influential in politics than it would sometimes seem.

Social and economic issues in the USA: health and housing

The idea of the 'American Dream' suggests that there are opportunities for all American citizens to prosper and experience a comfortable, healthy lifestyle. However, this is not always the case in reality. Inequality is a continued problem facing the USA and affects citizens in a variety of different ways.

Health and healthcare

Unlike the UK, there is no national health service in the USA. American citizens have been, until recently, responsible for meeting the cost of healthcare when they require it. This has led to extensive inequalities in relation to health and access to healthcare.

A significant number of Americans receive health insurance as part of their employment package (56% in 2017 according to the US Census Bureau); however, this has decreased in recent years. Others are entitled to government health programmes such as Medicaid (17.9%) and Medicare (17.8%). However, this does not account for everyone, and in 2018, 8.5% of the population of the USA had no health cover of any kind.

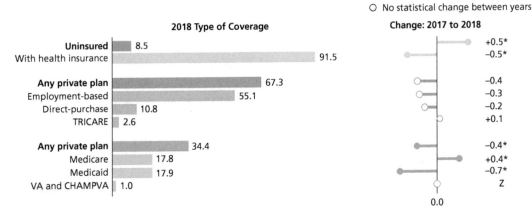

Percentage of people by type of health insurance coverage and change from 2017 to 2018

Even with the implementation of the Affordable Care Act (known as 'Obamacare'), there are still a huge number of uninsured American citizens. In 2018, the number of people in the United States without health insurance increased to 27.5 million, from 25.6 million in 2017. The uninsured rate increased from 7.9% in 2017 to 8.5% in 2018, which was the first increase in the number of uninsured people since 2008/9. Ethnic minorities were the least likely to be insured, with almost 16% of Hispanics having no arrangements for cover. Blacks and Asians were also less likely to be insured than Whites. This has an impact on children, with approximately 4.3 million children living without insurance in 2018. The consequences of this continue, with health issues growing throughout life, leading to lower life expectancy.

A recent report by the American Community Survey showed that since the introduction of Obmacare in 2010, the percentage of non-elderly uninsured fell from 17.8% to 10.2% in 2017, with the biggest winners being those aged between 18 and 34, Blacks, Hispanics and people who live in rural areas. The areas with the largest increases in coverage include rural Arkansas and Nevada, Southern Texas, large areas of New Mexico, Kentucky and West Virginia and many areas of California and Oregon.

It was hoped that health inequalities will decrease in time as a result of the Act, as currently ethnic minorities suffer poorer health overall and lower life expectancy. Black children for instance have twice the rate of infant mortality of White children. Although the number of uninsured had fallen steadily since the introduction of the Act, the latest figures for 2019 show the number rising again.

There is also evidence that ethnic minorities suffer disproportionate rates of health-related issues such as obesity, HIV and AIDS, with black women suffering the highest rates of death from lung cancer, heart disease and strokes.

Housing

Prior to the economic downturn in 2008, home ownership levels had reached their highest levels in history. Many Americans, including ethnic minorities, were able to afford to live in middle-class relatively crime-free suburbs. Many ethnic minorities had integrated into predominantly white neighbourhoods and were experiencing the benefits of suburban living – high quality housing and education with open spaces for children and families to enjoy. On the other hand, a significant number of Americans experience substandard housing, especially in the ghettos/barrios, where there are high rates of unemployment, poverty, violence and gang culture; the population of these areas are predominantly ethnic minorities. For example, Melrose-Morrisania, a borough of the Bronx, is the most deprived neighbourhood in New York; here, the majority of the population is Hispanic and mainly Puerto Rican and five low-income housing projects exist. In the Bronx overall, where according to the 2010 Census almost 90% of the population are of a minority ethnic group, 100 low-income housing projects exist, encompassing 44,500 apartments.

Homelessness

In the past, Americans were often homeless as a result of mental health issues or substance abuse. However, the economic crisis of 2008 resulted in thousands of Americans becoming unemployed and losing their homes because they had high-risk mortgages that they were no longer able to pay. Due to the lack of affordable housing, many Americans became homeless. With the demand for homeless accommodation outweighing the supply, a number of Americans resorted to temporary measures of accommodation, often referred to as 'tent cities'.

Temporary accommodation for the homeless

According to a 2018 report by the charity The National Alliance to End Homelessness, there were over 552,000 homeless people in the US. The report makes a clear reference to the relationship between homelessness and ethnic minorities, and the potential long-term impact. The report states, 'Gender and racial demographics are an important part of the American homelessness story. The homeless population is largely male. Among individual adults, 70% are men. White Americans are the largest racial grouping, accounting for 49% of those experiencing homelessness. However, African Americans and American Indians are dramatically overrepresented in the Point-in-Time Count compared to their numbers in the general population.' Children born into these situations will often find it very difficult to break this 'poverty cycle'.

> **TOP TIP**
>
> Read the following report by CNN detailing states with highest and lowest homelessness: https://edition.cnn.com/2019/06/06/us/homelessness-by-the-numbers/index.html

Quick Test

1. Describe what has happened to the number of people without health insurance in recent years.

2. List three pieces of evidence that indicate health inequalities for ethnic minorities.

3. What has led to the increasing numbers of homeless people in the USA?

Social and economic issues in the USA: education, employment and poverty

Education

Large numbers of Americans view education as the route to achieving the 'American Dream'. Most notably, Whites and Asians have the highest levels of success in education with Blacks and Hispanics less so, creating further long-term inequalities.

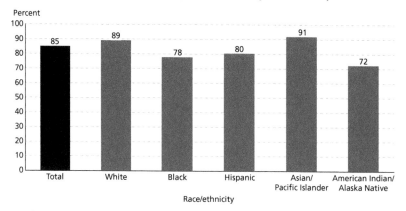

High school completion rates by race/ethnicity 2016/17

Asians are fast becoming the highest achievers with regard to education and outperform Whites on many occasions. However, even within this ethnic group there are inequalities – South Korean and Japanese young people do better than Cambodians and Vietnamese, for example. This is often as a result of stability in the household (higher levels of income on average, and cultures where a strong work ethic and education are valued) in the former groups.

The main reasons for these continuing inequalities are attributed to substandard schools and lack of resources, with the location of the school often being a major factor. Areas of deprivation, as noted above, have higher levels of ethnic minorities and often language barriers exist. Schools in these areas fail to attract and retain high performing students and teachers, ultimately leading to higher drop-out rates and poorer levels of attainment.

Dropout rates

The graph below shows the percentage of 18–24-year-olds who are not enrolled in school or have not earned a high school diploma.

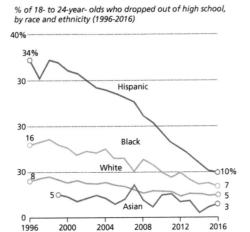

% of 18- to 24-year- olds who dropped out of high school, by race and ethnicity (1996-2016)

High school dropout rates 1996 - 2016

In each year, the dropout rate was lower for Whites than ethnic minorities and although the rates have declined for each group overall, there are still huge numbers of ethnic minorities with no formal qualification.

Poverty and unemployment

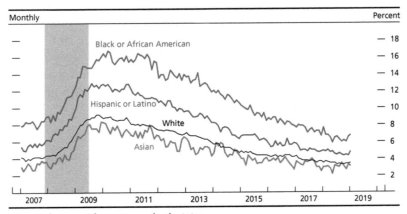

Unemployment by race and ethnicity

As the graph indicates, the unemployment rate in the USA has decreased in recent years; however, unemployment and the consequences of being unemployed vary within and between ethnic groups (see next page).

Unemployment rates by ethnic group in May 2019:

- White: 3.4%
- Black: 5.5%
- Hispanic: 4.2%
- Asian: 2.9%

According to the US Census Bureau, the official poverty rate in the USA in 2018 was 11.8% which represented a 3% fall in poverty since 2014 and was the first time the poverty rate was significantly lower since the 2008 financial crash. In 2018, there were 38.1 million people in poverty, approximately 1.4 million fewer people than 2017. Between 2017 and 2018, poverty rates for children under age 18 decreased by 1.2%.

The chart below highlights that Blacks have the highest levels of poverty, closely followed by Hispanics, with Whites and Asians less likely to live in poverty. As a result, Blacks and Hispanics are more likely to experience inequality. Why is this the case?

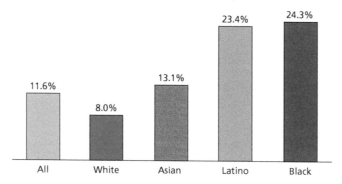

US poverty rates by ethnicity 2017

Black poverty

Black Americans have traditionally been the victims of racism and discrimination and as a result have often found it difficult to progress socially and economically. Many Black Americans live in ghettos and this is associated with limited opportunities in education, poorer healthcare and less chance of a fair trial; a disproportionately high level of convicted criminals in America are Black. In 2019, the Federal Bureau of Prisons annual report showed that Blacks made up 37.4% of the prison population although they make up only 13% of the total population of the USA.

Hispanic poverty

Different sub-groups within this ethnicity face different challenges. Mexicans and Puerto Ricans are more likely to live in poverty than Cubans.

Factors leading to poverty

- Unemployment
- Low educational attainment
- Discrimination
- Single-parent families
- Welfare cutbacks
- Poverty cycle

Poverty can often be attributed to low income. In 2017, it was clear that Blacks and Hispanics earned far less than Whites; however, the growing income of the Asian population was evident (see figure below).

Real Median Household Income by Race and Hispanic Origin: 1967 to 2017

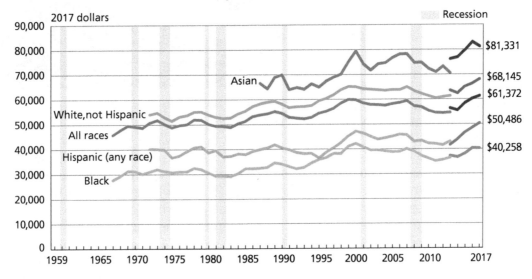

TOP TIP

Visit the website of Poverty USA to gain a more detailed understanding of the issue: http://www.povertyusa.org/facts

Quick Test

1. Outline the main reasons given for continuing inequalities in relation to education.
2. Using the information in the tables on pages 148 and 149, draw a conclusion about the link between ethnicity and educational attainment.
3. Using the figures above, what evidence is there that Blacks and Hispanics continue to face higher levels of inequality and poverty?

Social and economic issues in the USA: immigration

Immigration in the USA

Immigration is, and always will be an issue that deeply divides American citizens. This was never more evident than in the 2016 Presidential campaign when candidate Trump pledged to 'build a wall' to prevent what he said were unacceptable levels of illegal immigration across the USA–Mexico border. In 2018, the US Census Bureau calculated that 13.8% of the population were 'foreign born'. The top countries of origin were Mexico

Immigration continues to be an issue that deeply divides American citizens

(11.2%), China (2.9%), India (2.6%), Philippines (2%) and El Salvador (1.4%). It should be noted, however, that as far back as the 1890s almost 15% of the population was foreign born, mostly from European countries. The top US states where legal permanent residents settle are California (24%), Texas (11%) and New York (10%). In June 2019, 104,350 illegal immigrants were arrested or gave themselves up to the authorities at the US–Mexico border. This represented a decrease on the previous month and continued the downward trend from 2007. In recent years, the USA has witnessed a shift in attitude to immigration with recent legislation appearing to signify a more stringent approach. Increases in border security and the introduction of the US Patriot Act have all come out of this shift. Since he came to power, President Trump has implemented a number of policies and promises:

- To build a border 'wall' (or more accurately, 'barrier') between the USA and Mexico.
- Banned nationals of eight countries, mostly majority-Muslim, from entering the USA.
- Reduced refugee admissions to the lowest level since the resettlement program was created in 1980.
- Increased arrests of unauthorised immigrants in the USA.
- Canceled the Deferred Action for Childhood Arrivals (DACA) programme (sometimes referred to as the 'Dreamers' progamme), which allowed some unauthorised immigrants who had arrived as children, to stay and work temporarily.
- Ended the Temporary Protected Status for nationals of Haiti, Nicaragua and Sudan.

President Trump has made the border 'wall' a key policy

Continued immigration

Arguments for:	Arguments against:
• Contribution to the economy.	• Burden on the economy.
• Source of cheap labour.	• Poorly paid workers – keep wages low.
• Enterprise culture.	• Demise of 'American culture'.
• Cultural diversity.	• Terrorism.

TOP TIP

The issue of Immigration is likely to be a key issue in upcoming Presidential and Congressional elections. To understand its growing importance, look at the results of this 2019 Gallup opinion poll: https://news.gallup.com/poll/259103/new-high-say-immigration-important-problem.aspx.

Quick Test

1. From where do the majority of immigrants to the USA come?
2. How many 'unauthorised' immigrants are estimated to be living in the USA?
3. Describe the trend in unauthorised immigration since 2007.

Government responses to socio-economic inequalities

America First / Make America Great Again

Since he took office in January 2017, President Trump, as part of his 'America First' policy has implemented measures that he said would increase jobs and pay, including:

- Tax reductions for middle and high earners and businesses and cutting regulations for business to 'stimulate' the economy and create more jobs.
- Ending 'unfair' trade practices. He believed that countries such as China had been involved in 'unfair trading practices' that harmed American jobs. Starting in July 2018, he imposed tariffs on a wide range of Chinese goods to 'force' China to change these practices.
- Immigration control. Reducing the number of legal and illegal immigrants, the President believed, would protect jobs for Americans and help to protect wage levels as undocumented immigrants often work for less pay.

The evidence as to how successful these polcies have been is not always clear, for example:

- In 2019, unemployment in the USA had fallen to 3.6%; however, it had already been falling steadily since 2010.
- During President Trump's first 30 months in office, 5.74 million jobs were created. In the 30 months prior to his presidency, there were 6.61 million jobs created.
- In 2019, average wages were at their highest level since the 1970s; however, wages had been rising steadily since the mid 1990s.

Affordable Care Act – 'Obamacare'

In March 2010, President Obama signed the Affordable Care Act. This law put in place comprehensive health insurance reforms, aiming to extend health insurance coverage to some of the estimated 16% of the US population who lacked it. The Affordable Care Act was intended to make healthcare more affordable, accessible and of a higher quality for families, the elderly, businesses, and taxpayers alike. This includes previously uninsured Americans and Americans who had insurance that didn't provide them with adequate coverage and security.

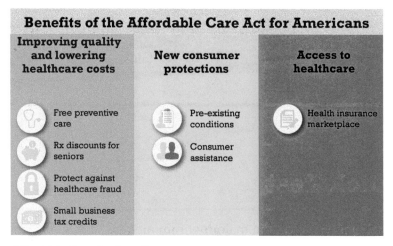

Benefits of the Affordable Care Act for Americans

Improving quality and lowering healthcare costs
- Free preventive care
- Rx discounts for seniors
- Protect against healthcare fraud
- Small business tax credits

New consumer protections
- Pre-existing conditions
- Consumer assistance

Access to healthcare
- Health insurance marketplace

Affordable Care Act benefits

This website highlights the key features of the Act year by year: www.hhs.gov/healthcare/facts/timeline/timeline-text.html

The law requires all Americans to have health insurance but offers subsidies to make coverage more affordable and aims to reduce the cost of insurance by bringing younger, healthier people into the health insurance system. By 2018, according to figures released by the Centre for Disease Control & Prevention, over 20 million more people had signed up for medical insurance since the launch of the Affordable Care Act (ACA) in 2010. During his election campaign, candidate Trump promised to get rid of Obamacare. He claimed that it had pushed up the cost of healthcare as insurers now had to cover more people and it had reduced competition between insurance providers as many had 'pulled out' of the Obamacare scheme. Although he failed on several occasions to get the ACA repealed, he has managed to scrap the 'individual shared responsibility provision' that compelled people who were not exempt to have health cover or pay a fine to help pay for the provision of healthcare.

Medicare and Medicaid

Medicaid, unlike the Affordable Care Act (Obamacare), is designed to offer either free, or low-cost healthcare coverage to those in need. While the ACA is done through the federal government, Medicaid is administered by individual states, which means the regulations might be different according to each state's laws. People who might be eligible for Medicaid include:

- Pregnant mothers
- Parent of a minor
- People with disabilities
- Low income earners

In 2018, 75.8 million people were covered by Medicaid.

Medicare is designed to help people over the age of 65, and with some younger people who have certain disabilities. Although recipients might have to pay a premium, the main cost of Medicare is paid for throughout a person's working life by deductions taken from their wages. Currently, Medicare covers:

- Part of the cost of hospital care
- Tests and procedures while in the hospital
- Prescription drugs

In 2018, over 60.8 million people were covered by Medicare.

Temporary Assistance for Needy Families (TANF)

Designed to help needy families achieve self-sufficiency, this programme sees states being given money from the US government in the form of a block grant. They are then given the task of creating welfare programmes that accomplish at least one of the four purposes of TANF:

- To provide assistance to needy families so that children can be cared for in their own homes.
- To reduce the dependency of needy parents by promoting job preparation, work and marriage.
- To prevent and reduce the incidence of out-of-wedlock pregnancies.
- To encourage the formation and maintenance of two-parent families.

In Washington, TANF provides temporary cash and medical help for families in need. Other families participate in the WorkFirst Program, which aims to help families find and keep jobs. The WorkFirst Program assists by helping pay for childcare expenses through the Child Care Subsidy Program. It also helps with completing applications and sometimes can provide training to help the unemployed back into work.

TANF's Reach Declined Significantly Over Time

Number of families receiving AFDC/TANF benefits for every 100 families with children in poverty

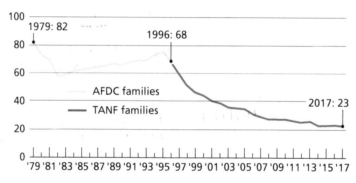

By 2017 the number of families receiving TANF had fallen by two thirds since it was started in 1996

TANF is based on family size and income. A family of three in Washington with no income would receive a monthly TANF grant of $569. As of August 1997, TANF families are limited to five years of benefits in their lifetime unless they qualify for a time limit extension. The graph (above) highlights the decline in TANF recipients – a direct result of the time limit being introduced.

Every Student Succeeds Act

The Every Student Succeeds Act (ESSA) passed in 2015 replaced the 'No Child Left Behind' policy. ESSA is the main education law for all public schools in the USA. It is intended to make sure schools are held accountable for providing a good quality education for all pupils including disadvantaged students in four main groups: students in poverty, minorities, students who receive special education and those with limited English language skills.

The responsibility for operating the policy falls to each individual state to decide how to best implement it. Each state, however, must:

- ensure they set clear and 'challenging' standards for what is to be learned at each stage
- carry out annual testing in literacy and maths
- regular testing in science
- have clear plans to support struggling schools to reach the expected standards
- publish 'report cards' for the state and its local school to ensure the public have information on how schools are doing.

Since ESSA was only put in place fully in 2016, it is difficult to gauge its success, but, as outlined previously (see pages 148–149), the levels of educational achievement in the USA have been improving for many years; however, there is still a significant gap between the attainment of different ethnic groups.

Supplemental Nutrition Assistance Program (SNAP)

SNAP offers nutritional support to low-income individuals and families as well as their communities. Those eligible receive assistance through an Electronic Benefit Transfer (EBT) card. Benefits are automatically loaded into the household's account each month. People use the SNAP EBT card to buy groceries at authorised food stores. The card works like a bank debit card. The cost of the eligible food items is deducted from the household's account automatically. SNAP can be used to buy foods such as

The SNAP card is accepted where this sign is displayed

bread and cereals, fruit and vegetables, meat, fish and poultry and dairy products. The benefit can also be used to buy seeds and plants that produce food for the household to eat. SNAP cannot, however, be used to buy any alcohol, cigarettes or tobacco; nor any nonfood items, such as pet foods, soaps, paper products and household supplies. In 2018, according to the United States Department of Agriculture, 40 million households were in receipt of SNAP. Two-thirds of those receiving SNAP are elderly, disabled or children. A recent report by the White House Council of Economic Advisers said that SNAP had a range of benefits, including:

- Improved birth weight and neonatal health
- Improved school performance
- More medical checkups and fewer hospital visits

TOP TIP

To find out more about the main welfare programmes in the USA, read this article from the financial website, The Balance: https://www.thebalance.com/welfare-programs-definition-and-list-3305759

Quick Test

1. Describe the main policies introduced by President Trump in the hope of 'stimulating the economy'.
2. What are the key purposes of the TANF and SNAP programmes?
3. Which groups of people may be covered by Medicare and Medicaid?

The role of the USA in international relations

The Role of the USA in the UN, NATO and the G7

The USA is still regarded as the world's dominant military, economic, social and political power. As a results, the USA plays a crucial role in each of the international organisations discussed in this chapter.

United Nations

The United Nations websites states: 'The United Nations is an international organization founded in 1945. It is currently made up of 193 Member States … Due to the powers vested in its charter and its unique international character, the United Nations can take action on many of the issues confronting humanity in the 21st century, such as peace and security, climate change, sustainable development, human rights, disarmament, terrorism, humanitarian and health emergencies, gender equality, governance, food production, and more.

Flag of the United Nations

The UN also provides a forum for its members to express their views in the General Assembly, the Security Council, the Economic and Social Council, and other bodies and committees. By enabling dialogue between its members, and by hosting negotiations, the organization has become a mechanism for governments to find areas of agreement and solve problems together.'

Power and influence of USA within the UN
- UN Headquarters is in a US city: New York City.
- The USA is estimated to contribute approximately 22% of the UN's annual budget due to the UN's ability-to-pay scale.
- Permanent member of the Security Council – primary responsibility for the maintenance of international peace and security.
- Under the UN Charter, all member states must comply with Security Council decisions.
- Has the power of veto.

Conflict between US and other member states
Since becoming President, Donald Trump has repeatedly stated his intention to put 'America First'. He believes that international organisations such as the United Nations and NATO reduce the USA's 'independence' to act in the best interests of America. In his

address to the United Nations General Assembly in 2018, he said, 'America will always choose independence and cooperation over global governance, control, and domination.' He has expressed several concerns about the UN and the USA's role in it, including:

- The USA contributes over one-fifth of the UN budget. He believed this was unfair, although the amount each country pays depends on its wealth and population.
- The UN was not taking a strong enough stance against countries he argued were a serious threat, including Iran.
- In his first address to the UN in 2017, he told the General Assembly the UN was not doing enough to stop North Korea's 'relentless pursuit' of nuclear weapons. In his speech, he stated that if the USA 'is forced to defend itself or its allies, we will have no choice but to totally destroy North Korea'.
- The UN's focus on climate change was making demands that were harmful to American industry.

In response to these concerns about international bodies like the UN reducing the USA's right to act in its own best interests, President Trump has:

- Withdrawn from the Paris Climate Agreement, which aims to tackle climate change, because it 'will undermine the US economy and puts the US at a permanent disadvantage'.
- Withdrawn from the Joint Comprehensive Plan of Action (the 'Iran Deal') which was set up to control Iran's nuclear production in return for lifting sanctions. He believed Iran was 'secretly' breaking the agreement and was supporting terrorism abroad.
- Reduced or stopped funding for some UN agencies; for example, the agency responsible for Palestinian refugees, because the Palestinians would not drop their demands for the 'right to return' to land in Israel that they claimed had been taken from them.

NATO

NATO's essential purpose is to safeguard the freedom and security of its members through political and military means. The USA has been a member of NATO since 1949 and it is often referred to as the Atlantic Alliance, creating a situation whereby the security of the US and Europe is linked.

NATO as an organisation is responsible for:

- Decisions and consultations
- Operations and missions
- Partnerships
- Developing the means to respond to threats

The compass rose emblem of NATO

The US has a vital role to play. US troops are deployed in more than 150 countries around the world with approximately 160,000 of its active-duty personnel serving outside the United States and its territories, and an additional 170,000 deployed in various contingency operations.

President Trump and NATO

Although he has been critical of NATO members for, as he sees it, relying too much on the USA to fund NATO and provide the bulk of its military, President Trump has actually increased the USA's involvement by:

- Contributing to and leading new 'rapid reaction' battalions in Eastern Europe to counter Russian aggression in the area.
- Planning to spend over $800m in 2019 in Eastern Europe to improve NATO's ability to respond quickly to Russian aggression, especially using aircraft.
- Continuing many of the military operations started under previous Presidents, including Afghanistan, Iraq, Syria and Yemen.

G7

Until 2014, the eight most powerful countries in the world were known as the G8 – Canada, France, Germany, Italy, Japan, Russia, the UK and the USA. It aims to tackle global issues through discussions at the annual G8 summit. In 2014, the G8 summit was suspended as a result of the Crimean crisis and Russia has since been excluded from the G8 countries. The remaining seven countries (the G7) continue to meet annually. President Trump has expressed disagreement with the G7 on several occasions, including the exclusion of Russia, which

The flags of the original G8 member states

he thinks should be readmitted. He also chose not to attend meetings considering climate change and in 2018, he refused to sign the final agreement following a disagreement with Canadian Prime Minister Justin Trudeau over trade tariffs.

Quick Test

1. List three key features that highlight the power and influence the US has in the UN.
2. Describe how recent issues have caused conflict between the US and other UN member states.
3. What evidence is there that the USA is actually increasing its involvement with NATO in Europe?
4. What objections has President Trump expressed about the work of the G7?

Terrorism

Internationally, there is no agreed definition of terrorism; however, the UK Terrorism Act (2000) defines terrorism as:

'The use or threat of action designed to influence the government or an international governmental organisation or to intimidate the public, or a section of the public; made for the purposes of advancing a political, religious, racial or ideological cause; and it involves or causes:

- Serious violence against a person.
- Serious damage to a property.
- A threat to a person's life.
- A serious risk to the health and safety of the public.
- Serious interference with or disruption to an electronic system.'

In more recent years, countries worldwide have witnessed increasing terrorist threats and attacks and terrorism continues to pose a serious and sustained problem for all those involved. As a result of this continued threat, the UK government publicises the level of threat they believe the UK is under, in order for the UK public to remain alert to potential attacks. This publication of information came in the aftermath of the 7 July, 2005 attack on the London transport system.

Threat levels

- **Low** – an attack is unlikely.
- **Moderate** – an attack is possible, but not likely.
- **Substantial** – an attack is a strong possibility.
- **Severe** – an attack is highly likely.
- **Critical** – an attack is expected imminently.

The threat level from international terrorism was raised to severe in the UK in August 2014 and has remained at this level or higher. This threat level is continually monitored and reviewed by government agencies, based on intelligence gathered and terrorist activities occurring in the international community. Assessments of the international threat level are made by the Joint Terrorism Analysis Centre, while the UK Security Service is responsible for setting the threat levels for Irish and other domestic terrorism. Since September 2010, the threat levels for Northern Ireland-related terrorism have also been made available.

The colour-coded threat levels

Quick Test

1. Where does the UK outline its definition of terrorism?
2. List the five main outcomes that could occur as a result of a terrorist attack.
3. Why does the UK government publicise the threat level for international terrorism?

Causes of terrorism

It is evident that the causes of terrorism and terrorist activities are varied, and it is widely recognised that those committing terrorist acts are doing so for a particular cause or purpose, coercing society into change by attracting attention and public acknowledgement of their cause by means of intimidation, threat and violence.

Four key causes

Social and political injustice
Terrorists act on the assumption that they believe they have been stripped of something they are entitled to, such as certain rights or access to land.

Religious beliefs
Religious causes have been the motivation for a number of terrorist attacks. Terrorists in these situations believe they are avenging what they perceive as an attack on their religious beliefs. We have to be mindful of the fact that it is not always one religion attacking another; attacks in Northern Ireland that were linked to the troubles between Protestants and Catholics are a clear example of this, given that both groups would be regarded as Christians.

Ideological beliefs
A number of groups have engaged in terrorism to advance the ideology they believe in, which is not necessarily political or religious, e.g. animal rights campaigners, 'eco terrorists' and racist groups. Currently in the UK, the greatest threat from terrorism is most likely to come from Islamist and right-wing groups. Theresa May in the Foreword to The United Kingdom's Strategy for Countering Terrorism in 2018 wrote that the UK's Counter Terrorism Strategy had 'foiled 25 Islamist plots since June 2013, and four

ALF logo

extreme right-wing terror plots in the past year (2017) alone' and the UK's most senior counter-terrorism officer Neil Basu revealed at an international conference on terrorism in 2019 that the number of attacks foiled since the Westminster atrocity in March 2017 has risen to 22, with seven relating to suspected far-right terror.

Socio-economic factors
Deprivation and related factors such as poverty or a lack of education are now regarded as causes that can drive people to engage in terrorist activities. Researchers suggest that individuals in these situations may be easier to recruit as a result of their socio-economic status. Criminality also plays a part according to the Global Terrorism Index, which states that 'there is a growing body of evidence which indicates that people in Western Europe with a criminal background may be especially susceptible to alignment with extremist beliefs'.

Quick Test

1. Summarise the four key causes of terrorism.
2. What evidence is there to prove that religious attacks are not always one religion against another?
3. According to the UK government, what currently are the main sources of possible ideological terrorism?

Religious extremism

According to the Global Terrorism Index in 2017, the terrorist organisation Islamic State in the Levant (ISIL), also known as ISIS, 'remained the deadliest terrorist group globally'. Although the number of deaths caused by terrorism had fallen significantly from the high point of 2014, every region in the world recorded an increase in the impact from terrorism in 2017 compared to 2002.

Terrorist organisations

The majority of these attacks were attributed to four main terrorist organisations:

- Islamic State (ISIS) in Iraq and Syria
- Boko Haram in Nigeria
- Taliban in Afghanistan
- Al Shabab in Somalia and east Africa

According to Global Terrorism Index 2018, compiled by the Institute for Economics & Peace (IEP), these four organisations were responsible for 10,632 deaths in 2017. Their actions contribute to the instability of what are some of the most dangerous countries in the world, including Afghanistan, Iraq, Nigeria, Somalia and Syria. Over the past decade they have accounted for 44% of all terrorist deaths. In certain regions of Europe in the recent past there were acts of political terrorism by separatist groups who wanted to set up their own independent states; for example, the IRA and ETA. However, since these organisations declared ceasefires, this type of terrorism is much less common in Europe today.

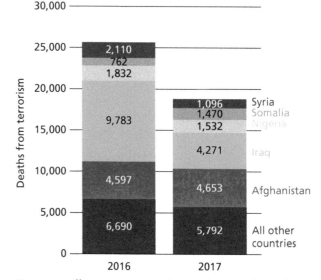

Terrorism affects some countries much more than others

Case study: Boko Haram

According to the Red Cross, since 2011, an estimated 35,000 have been killed and more than 2 million have been displaced by the terrorist group Boko Haram (its name means 'Western education is a sin' in the local language). It has also been responsible for mass kidnappings and the large-scale use of women and children as suicide bombers. It was once classed the world's deadliest terror group. It started in the north-east of Nigeria and spread its activities to the nearby countries of Chad, Cameroon and Niger. It has sworn loyalty to the Islamic State (ISIS). As a result of international action and the Nigerian security forces, the number of deaths has declined by 83% since 2014 and the group itself has split into different factions who have fought each other. Although killings have fallen, the figures for 2017 showed an increase in both attacks and deaths.

Boko Haram is strongest in Borno, Yobe and Adamawa

The Global Terrorism Index

The Global Terrorism Index allocates a rating to each country dependent on how affected they are by terrorism. The graph below highlights where each country rates in this index. While the UK and the USA have higher rates than Europe and North America (shown), they have lower ratings than countries regarded as suffering the highest impact of terrorism such as Nigeria, Pakistan and Afghanistan.

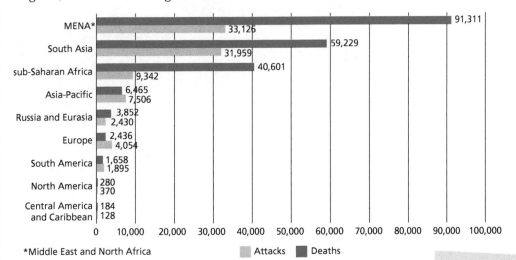

*Middle East and North Africa

Largest number of deaths were recorded in the MENA region, with over 90,000 deaths from terrorism since 2002

TOP TIP

Read the Key Findings from the Global Terrorism Index report for 2018 to find out more about terrorism around the world: http://visionofhumanity.org/app/uploads/2018/12/Global-Terrorism-Index-2018.pdf

Quick Test

1. 'Religious extremism is the main cause of deaths today.' What evidence is there to support this view?

2. To which organisations were the majority of religious attacks attributed?

3. Using the information on the previous pages, draw conclusions about:
   - Global terror attacks within certain countries in comparison to the rest of the world.
   - Trends in ideology-related incidents.

Issues for the future

Although the number of deaths from terrorism has declined since 2014, there are still very serious threats globally. Groups such as ISIS and Boko Haram may have lost influence in the conflict areas in which they operate, but the nature of terrorism is changing and newer threats such as online radicalisation and right-wing extremism continue to threaten violence.

The 'lone wolf'

This is someone who commits or is suspected of committing an act of terror in support of a recognised terrorist organisation or movement. The difference is that they normally do so without any financial or material help from such groups. It is often argued that a lone wolf represents a greater threat to countries than organised movements, given that individuals could go undetected as they actually may never come into contact with the group they support.

- On 3 August 2019, Patrick Crusius, a lone gunman entered a Walmart store in El Paso, Texas armed with an assault weapon and began firing indiscriminately on the shoppers inside, killing 20 people and injuring a further 26. Shortly before the attack, Crusius had posted racist and anti-immigrant statements online and gave as his reason the intention to 'stop the Hispanic invasion of Texas'. The US Attorney for the Western District of Texas classed the attack as a 'domestic terrorist case'.

- In May of 2017, an extreme islamist terrorist, Salman Abedi blew himself up using a home-made bomb in the Manchester Arena at the end of an Ariana Grande concert. 23 people were killed and a further 139 were injured. Most of the dead and injured were young people attending the concert. Albedi was British-born, of Libyan ancestry.

Terrorist cells

A cell is a very small group of terrorists operating together in a specific area. They are often referred to as the 'building blocks' for a larger network or terrorist organisation. The cell may be linked only to a group leader and may be completely unaware of other cells operating close by. In Germany in March 2019, 10 people were arrested in the states of Hesse and Rhineland-Palatinate. They were found guilty of intending to 'kill as many "non-believers" as possible' using guns and vehicles. Seven of the group were German nationals.

Home-grown terrorism

Home-grown terrorism or domestic terrorism is associated with acts of violence committed by citizens of the same country they attack. In a bid to instill terror in the people and government of France, brothers Said and Cherif Kouachi attacked the staff of the *Charlie Hebdo* magazine in Paris in January 2015, killing 11 people and injuring 11 others. Shortly afterwards they killed a policeman. The attacks were in response to the publication of satirical cartoons of the prophet Muhammad.

The Charlie Hebdo building in Paris was attacked in January 2015

Quick Test

1. Why is a 'lone wolf' regarded as a significant threat to security?
2. Why are terrorist cells referred to as 'building blocks'?
3. Why could the Manchester Arena attacks and the Walmart shootings be described as 'home-grown terrorism'?

Consequences of terrorist activities: individuals

Individuals

Terrorism at its most extreme can cause loss of a loved one or an entire family, and the threat of continued terrorist attacks induces fear in individuals worldwide. This fear can often result in irrational behaviour, such as fear of flying or the potential to feel under threat for your safety. In addition, individuals can develop a hatred of certain groups or individuals; for example, 'Islamophobia', threatening the rights afforded to individuals. In July of 2018, the University of Manchester produced a study in which they found that the UK government's 'Prevent Strategy' to tackle extremism made young Muslims feel like a 'suspect community'. The report's author Professor Hilary Pilkington said that the policy was seen by many young Muslims as reinforcing the association some people made between Islam and terrorism.

Research indicates that a certain number of individuals are at risk of radicalisation. In January 2018, the University College London (UCL) published research which showed that one of the main factors in radicalisation among young Muslim men in Europe was social exclusion and isolation, which created a sense of inequality and discrimination. The study questioned previous explanations that pointed to things like poverty, as there were many examples of young middle-class people who had been radicalised.

Case study: Aqsa Mahmood

Privately educated, Aqsa Mahmood left her Glasgow home in November 2013 to join ISIS in Syria, where she married an Islamic State (ISIS) fighter. She told her parents she wanted to become a martyr and would see them again on the 'day of judgment'.

She was later suspected of helping other young women to travel to Syria to become 'Jihadi brides' including the so-called 'Bethnal Green Trio', one of whom, Shamima Begum, tried and failed to be readmitted to the UK in 2019.

Children

Those children who are directly and indirectly involved in terrorism can be particularly vulnerable. Children living in areas where terrorist activities are frequent are at risk of suffering a number of damaging and life-changing experiences, from injury through to losing parents or even death. Furthermore, the American Psychological Association (APA) argue that children are at risk of experiencing mental health difficulties after an act of terrorism. Following the Manchester Arena bombing, the Royal College of Psychiatrists found that there had been a significant increase in the demand for mental health support from young people who were caught up in the incident. Dr Louise Theodosiou from the Manchester Children's Hospital said the attack had a 'profound impact on the way the children view their city'.

Children of Gaza

The region of Gaza, sometimes referred to as the Gaza strip, is a Palestinian controlled area that has been at the centre of the long-running dispute between Israelis and Palestinians in the Middle East. In May 2018, the United Nations International Children's Fund (UNICEF) Regional Director for the Middle East and North Africa, issued a statement highlighting the suffering of the children of Gaza as a result of the conflict. According to UNICEF, half the children needed humanitarian aid to survive and one in four needed psychosocial care due to severe distress and trauma. Because of the damage done to many schools, those that remained were doing treble shifts and nine out of ten families with children did not have regular access to clean, safe drinking water.

Palestinian children salvage items from the rubble of destroyed buildings in part of Gaza City's al-Tufah neighbourhood

TOP TIP

Follow the link below to read a report by Child Soldiers International, about children used as soldiers in conflicts around the world: https://reliefweb.int/sites/reliefweb.int/files/resources/CSI_annual_report_2018.pdf

Quick Test

1. List three ways that terrorism can affect individuals.
2. Outline the problems faced by children as a result of terrorism. Give evidence to support your answer.

Consequences of terrorist activities: countries and their governments

Economic consequences

Terrorism is not confined to one specific country or region, countries worldwide suffer the impact and consequences of terrorism. The Global Terrorism Index (GTI) states that the 'economic costs of terrorism go further than the destruction of property and the loss of life. The increased costs of security, military expenditure and insurance often outweigh the original attack'. These can be categorised into **primary (direct)** and **secondary (indirect)** costs.

Primary (direct) costs:	Secondary (indirect) costs:
• Immediate damage caused. • Loss of life, injury. • Damage to infrastructure.	• Disruptions to economy due to event/threat. • Increased security costs. • Decrease in foreign investment. • Decreased trade. • Decreased tourism.

In 2018, the Rand Corporation issued its study into the cost of terrorism in Europe. It estimated that the 28 EU states had lost about €180 billion between 2004 and 2016 with the largest costs to the UK (€43.7bn), France (€43bn) and Spain (€40.8bn). Although the negative effects on things such as consumer spending and tourism were not long lasting, there were several ongoing costs associated with terrorism including government spending to repair damaged infrastructure, increased security arrangements, adapting buildings to prevent attacks etc. In the UK in 2017 alone the attacks in Westminster, Manchester, London Bridge, Finsbury Park and Parsons Green were estimated to have cost £3.5bn in lost economic output and following these attacks Amber Rudd, the then Home Secretary, announced an additional £24m was to be spend on anti-terrorism policing.

Social consequences

Countries, as well as individuals, may suffer the social consequences of terrorism in relation to an increase in fear, homelessness and poverty. Yemen, ranked 6th in the Global Terrorism Index list in 2019 of countries worst affected by terrorism, is a clear example of the link between terrorism and poverty. The World Bank highlighted Yemen as the poorest country in the Arab world in 2019, with the poverty rate increasing from 42% in 2009 to an estimated 71–78% in 2019 and being one of the most food-insecure countries globally, with the UN World Food Programme highlighting that 'approximately 56% of Yemen's population will experience Crisis (IPC 3) or worse levels of acute food insecurity through early 2020'. It is estimated that more than 40% of households have lost their main source of income and find it increasingly difficult to afford the minimum food requirements. Unemployment is very high with the World Bank estimating youth unemployment at almost 1 in 4, which links back to the fact that young men and women are vulnerable targets for religious extremists. In fact, there has been an increase in the activities of Al Qaeda and ISIL in Yemen in recent years. This could suggest that terrorism contributes to a cyclical pattern of poverty – those in poverty resort to terrorist measures as a response to the poverty they live in, in turn causing further devastation and destruction.

The World Bank highlighted Yemen as one of the poorest countries in the Arab world

Countries such as Japan, however, have been virtually free from international terrorism, only suffering a small number of attacks, mainly as a result of home-grown terrorists acting against the government.

Although Japan experiences very few terrorist incidents – it is ranked at 58th out of 76 in the Global Terrorism Index – there is still a threat. On New Year's Day 2019, a 21-year-old man drove his car at pedestrians, injuring nine people, some seriously. The young man claimed he did it to protest against the execution of the leader of Aum Shinrikyo and 12 of his followers.

Case study: Islamic State (ISIS)

Supporters of ISIS

ISIS (also known as Islamic State in Iraq and the Levant (ISIL) and Islamic State (IS)) is a Jihadist terrorist group. When it was set up in April 2013, its leader Abu Bakr al-Baghdadi declared its aim to establish a 'caliphate' across Iraq, Syria and beyond. As a result of large-scale military attacks, by 2014 it controlled 34,000 square miles of territory in Iraq and Syria. Tens of thousands have travelled to Iraq and Syria to join ISIS from around the world – one estimate by Kings College London puts the figure at over 40,000. By 2019, international action against ISIS, including a US-led Combined Joint Task Force, meant ISIS had lost most of its territory and did not control any major centres of population. However, the Pentagon has warned that it is 'resurging' in Syria following US troops' withdrawal.

ISIS – a changing threat

ISIS is still in control of large funds of money that it is believed, by security forces around the world, will be used to fund further terrorist attacks by 'lone operators' or small cells. The Global Terrorism Index of 2018 states: 'More troubling, is the potential for many hardened fighters and leaders to leave Iraq and Syria to join new radical permutations of ISIL or existing ISIL affiliates in other countries'.

Quick Test

1. Outline the difference between primary and secondary costs of terrorism.
2. Explain what is meant by 'ongoing costs' of terrorism to an economy.
3. What are the three main social consequences of terrorism?
4. Why might conditions in Yemen explain the increase in the activities of groups such as Al Qaeda and ISIS in recent years?
5. In what way might the actions of ISIS change following its losses in Iraq and Syria?

International community

In recent years, the international community has had to respond to a number of terrorist attacks, impacting on a number of countries, both directly and indirectly. As a result, there is agreement that international terrorism and the threat of further attacks have huge consequences for the international community.

Case study: Arab Spring

In December 2010, Mohamed Bouazizi, a young Tunisian man, was stopped by police from selling fruit in the street. He set himself on fire in protest. A few weeks later he died; however, his actions encouraged an uprising that saw the downfall of President Ben Ali and paved the way for a number of uprisings and revolutions across the Middle East.

In Egypt, after 18 days of mass protest, President Mubarak was forced to resign after 29 years in power. Anti-government demonstrations in Libya started what was to be the downfall and ultimate death of Colonel Gaddafi after 42 years in power. Although not a terrorist threat in essence, it had a major impact on the international community, with the UN Security Council authorising 'all necessary measures' to protect civilians. NATO launched military attacks as well as imposing a no-fly zone.

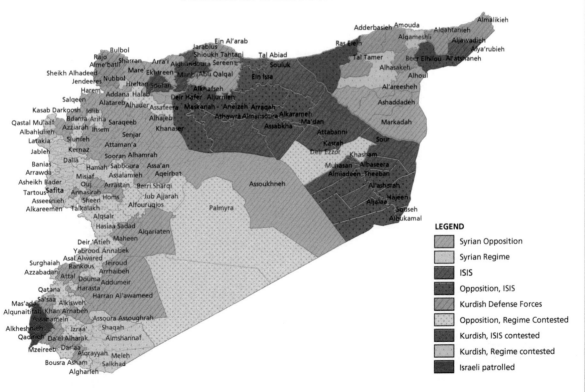

SYRIA TERRITORY MAP: AUG. 31,2014

LEGEND
- Syrian Opposition
- Syrian Regime
- ISIS
- Opposition, ISIS
- Kurdish Defense Forces
- Opposition, Regime Contested
- Kurdish, ISIS contested
- Kurdish, Regime contested
- Israeli patrolled

Isis controlled large areas of Syria after the Arab Spring

Many of the countries affected by the Arab Spring in the Middle East and North Africa (MENA) had repressive and corrupt regimes in which the people were denied rights and often suffered low standards of living. Those taking part in the uprisings hoped it would lead to improved living standards and increased democracy; however, the regimes responded with force and further repression. Civil wars and other conflicts resulted in groups such as Al Qaeda and ISIS taking advantage of this instability, spreading their influence throughout the region.

Quick Test

1. Outline the events of the uprisings in the Middle East, also referred to as the Arab Spring.
2. Use the following link to read an assessment of the impact of the Arab Spring on the rise of terrorist groups: https://www.theguardian.com/world/2018/dec/30/arab-spring-aftermath-syria-tunisia-egypt-yemen-libya

Resolving terrorism: national attempts

In the UK

Since 2014, the UK terror threat level has been at 'severe' or higher – meaning a terrorist attack is highly likely. It is the responsibility of the UK government to protect UK citizens, with the Home Office being the department challenged with this difficult task. A range of measures are in place in an attempt to counter the threat of terrorism.

Home Secretary, Priti Patel

CONTEST

The Office for Security and Counter-Terrorism works to counter the threat from terrorism by carrying out the government's counter-terrorism strategy, 'CONTEST'.

The strategy is based on four areas of work:

- Pursue – to stop terrorist attacks.
- Prevent – to stop people becoming terrorists or supporting terrorism.
- Protect – to strengthen our protection against a terrorist attack.
- Prepare – to mitigate the impact of a terrorist attack.

The Home Office report that they are:

- Carrying out a communications capabilities development programme, which will give them the ability to continue to protect the public in the future, as internet-based communications become increasingly widespread.
- Using science and technology to counter the threat from terrorism.
- Supporting the UK security industry to export their products and expertise to other countries hosting major international events.
- Working with the Northern Ireland Office and the relevant authorities in Northern Ireland to help counter the severe threat from terrorism in Northern Ireland.

Legislation

The UK government has also passed a number of pieces of legislation in a bid to counter terrorism.

Prevention of Terrorism Act (2005)

This Act established the 'control order' – a form of house arrest.

Terrorism Act (2006)

- Drawn up in the wake of the 7 July bomb attacks in London.
- Attempt to disrupt the training and recruitment of potential terrorists.
- Tony Blair suffered his first Commons defeat as PM when attempting to extend the time police could detain terror suspects without charge to 90 days – parliament agreed in the end to increase the time from 14 days to 28.

The Counter-Terrorism Act (2008)

- Enables police to take fingerprints and DNA samples from individuals subject to control orders.
- Enables police to enter – by force if necessary – and search the premises of individuals subject to control orders.
- Enables the Treasury to direct the financial sector to take action on suspected money laundering or terrorist financing.

Terrorism Prevention and Investigation Measures Act (2011)

- Abolished control orders.
- Introduced 'Terrorism Prevention and Investigation Measures' (TPIMs) – similar to control orders and include the following measures:
  - Electronic tagging, reporting regularly to the police.
  - Living at home, unable to leave overnight.
- TPIMs expire after a maximum of two years unless new evidence emerges of involvement in terrorism.

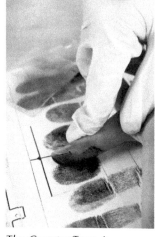

The Counter-Terrorism Act (2008) enabled police to take fingerprints from people under control orders

Protection of Freedoms Act (2012)

- Repealed the stop and search powers and replaced them with fairer and more specific powers, enabling the police to protect the public but also make sure that there are strong safeguards to prevent a return to the previous excessive use of stop and search without suspicion.
- Reduced the maximum period that a terrorist suspect could be detained before they are charged or released from 28 to 14 days.

Counter-Terrorism and Security Act (2015)

- Strengthened powers to place temporary restrictions on travel where a person is suspected of involvement in terrorism.
- Enhanced existing Terrorism Prevention and Investigation Measures to monitor and control the actions of individuals in the UK who pose a threat.
- Extended the retention of relevant communications data to help to identify individuals in the who pose a threat.

- Strengthened security arrangements in relation to the border and to aviation, maritime and rail transport.
- Deradicalistion programmes.

Counter-Terrorism and Border Security Act (2019)

- Updates terrorism offences for the digital age, and to reflect contemporary patterns of radicalisation.
- Disrupts terrorism by enabling the police to intervene at an earlier stage in investigations.
- Ensures that sentences properly reflect the seriousness of terrorism offences, and strengthen the ability of the police to manage terrorist offenders after their release.
- Strengthens the country's defences at the border against hostile state activity.

Quick Test

1. Outline the four areas of work upon which the CONTEST strategy is based.
2. Human rights groups have objected to parts of anti-terrorist legislation. Which parts of the legislation do you think they might object to? Explain your answer.
3. Visit the *Guardian* newspaper's website for a collection of articles about UK security and counter terrorism: https://www.theguardian.com/uk/uksecurity

Resolving terrorism: international attempts

USA

Immediately after 9/11, Congress passed a significant number of laws to support Bush's 'war on terror', outlined below.

- Authorisation for Use of Military Force (2001) – grants the President the authority to use all 'necessary and appropriate force' against those whom he determines 'planned, authorized, committed or aided' the September 11th attacks, or who harboured those persons or groups.

- USA Patriot Act (2001) – broadened the discretion of law enforcement and immigration agencies to detain and deport suspected terrorists, while reducing existing restrictions related to intelligence gathering.

- Creation of Department of Homeland Security (2002) – responsibility for preventing terrorist attacks on the US.

- Military Commission Act (2007) – authorised trial by military commission for violations of the law of war, and for other purposes.

Guantanamo Bay is still in operation although much reduced

Further acts were introduced in relation to terror suspects, limitations on the detention of prisoners, definitions of torture and war crimes and during the Bush regime the US came under intense scrutiny around the treatment of detainees at Guantanamo Bay. When Obama came to power in 2009, he issued an executive order promising to close the controversial prison within a year; however, while he did manage to reduce the numbers from 245 to 41, his successor Donald Trump signed an executive order to keep it open 'indefinitely'.

Bureau of Counterterrorism (CT)

The US does, however, continue to fight the threat of terror with a National Strategy for Counterterrorism, part of the US Strategy for National Security, and also makes international attempts to resolve the issue through the Bureau of Counterterrorism, which aims to forge partnerships with different organisations and foreign governments to develop coordinated strategies to defeat terrorists and secure the cooperation of international partners.

Bureau of Counterterrorism: programmes and initiatives

Antiterrorism Assistance Programme – US antiterrorism training and equipment given to law-enforcement agencies of partner nations.

Countering the Financing of Terrorism Finance – freezing and blocking finances of terror groups and preventing others from helping them.

Counterterrorism Partnerships Fund – to build a network of partnerships from South Asia to the Sahel to develop more effective partnerships in countries and regions where terrorist networks seek to establish a foothold.

Foreign Emergency Support Team – to rapidly respond to terrorist incidents worldwide.

Global Counterterrorism Forum – promote civilian cooperation and good practices to counter terrorism. The GCTF is composed of 30 countries and the EU.

Terrorist Screening and Interdiction Programmes – terrorist suspects screening database shared with US agencies and foreign partners.

Modernisation of Executive Order 13224

Following the 9/11 attacks, the then President George Bush signed executive order 13224, which stated the intention of the USA to weaken terrorist groups by 'freezing the assets' (i.e. blocking any funds or property) of those who were linked to, supported or might commit acts of terrorism. This Executive Order was updated by President Trump in September of 2019 to give greater powers to target the assets of groups and individuals as well as those who participated in training to commit acts of terrorism. The order also warned financial institutions in the USA and abroad that they would face sanctions (punishment) from the USA if they conducted any financial transactions for any of the groups or people listed by the Order.

Quick Test

1. What evidence is there to argue that despite President Trump's 'America First' policy, the USA continues to work in partnership with other countries to counter terrorism?

2. Explain how Executive Order 13224 aims to weaken the ability of terrorist groups to carry out acts of terrorism.

The UN and NATO's responses to terrorism

UN Global Counter-Terrorism Strategy

At the 2005 World Summit, then UN Secretary-General Kofi Annan announced proposals for a comprehensive and effective approach to terrorism. Member states agreed, for the first time, on a clear and unqualified condemnation of terrorism and since then have continued to reiterate the need to uphold and promote the UN Global Counter-Terrorism Strategy, which encompasses four main elements:

- Tackling the conditions conducive to the spread of terrorism.
- Preventing and combating terrorism.
- Building states' capacity to prevent and combat terrorism.
- Ensuring respect for human rights and the rule of law as the fundamental basis of the fight against terrorism.

UN member states take a vote

As the main body safeguarding international law, the UN can play an important role in strengthening legal approaches to terrorism, with the UN Security Council in recent years strengthening the work of its counter-terrorism bodies.

In 2017 it established the UN Office of Counter-Terrorism. The main functions of the UNOCT are:

- to advise the General Assembly and coordinate the work of all UN agencies involved in counter terrorism
- to assist UN member states to strengthen their counter-terrorism strategies
- to ensure all UN agencies give priority to the UN Global Counter-Terrorism Strategy and the work being done to prevent violent extremism.

Following the September 11 attacks in the USA, the UN adopted the first wide-ranging Resolution 1373, which required all member states to respond to international terrorist threats by a range of measures including penalising acts of support for terrorism and freezing the funds of anyone planning or committing terrorist acts. Further resolutions include Resolution 2170 condemning human rights abuses in Iraq and Syria.

TOP TIP

Visit the website of the UN Office of Counter-Terrorism to find out more about the UN's counter-terrorism strategies: https://www.un.org/counterterrorism/ctitf/en/un-global-counter-terrorism-strategy

NATO

NATO recognises terrorism as a 'global threat that knows no border, nationality or religion – a challenge that the international community must tackle together'. NATO's counter-terrorism policy focuses on: improving awareness of the threat of terrorism; developing capabilities to prepare and respond to it; improving engagement with partner countries and other international actors.

NATO (OTAN in French)

NATO has been involved in several counter-terrorism operations in recent years, including:

- Its first ever counter-terrorism operation – Operation Eagle Assist – following the 9/11 terrorist attacks on the United States. (This was the first and only time Article 5 was put into operation where NATO members commit to protecting each other.)
- Patrolled the Mediterranean Sea on counter-terrorism missions since 2001 as part of Operations Active Endeavour and now Operation Sea Guardian.
- July 2018, NATO and the EU agreed to focus on making progress in the areas of military mobility, counter-terrorism and strengthening resilience to chemical, biological, radiological and nuclear-related risks.
- It has supported the Global Coalition to Defeat ISIS by supplying AWACS intelligence-gathering aircraft.
- It set up a regional hub for the south in Italy that helps it to anticipate and respond to crises arising in areas such as North Africa and Sahel, the Middle East, sub-Saharan Africa and adjacent areas.
- The Istanbul Cooperation Initiative (ICI) encourages countries in the wider Middle East to cooperate on security matters to counter terrorism.

TOP TIP

The NATO website has more detailed information on how the organisation is attempting to combat terrorism: www.nato.int/cps/en/natohq/topics_77646.htm

Quick Test

1. What are the four key elements of the UN Global Counter-Terrorism Strategy?
2. Outline the aims of the UN Office of Counter-Terrorism.
3. Explain the significance of Resolution 1373.
4. Gives examples of how both the UN and NATO work with partners to counter terrorism.

Effectiveness of measures to combat terrorism

Given the fact that terrorism and terrorist attacks occur on an international scale, we have to question how effective measures taken to combat terrorism actually are. We could argue that we have not witnessed anything on the scale of 9/11 again and therefore measures must be working; however, the constant threat and occurrence of radicalised groups and individuals would suggest that more should be done.

Case study: terror suspects travel to and return from Syria

As outlined previously, tens of thousands of people from all over the world travel to Iraq and Syria to join organisations such as ISIS. According to a House of Commons paper in March 2019, 'Returning Terrorist Fighters', the government estimated that approximately 900 people from the UK had travelled to Syria and Iraq to join terrorist groups, of which approximately 40% have returned. Of this number around 40 had been prosecuted so far because of their actions in Syria, or since they came back. Although the introduction of the Counter-Terrorism and Border Security Act 2019 gave more powers to prosecute returnees, Cressida Dick, the Commissioner of the Metropolitan Police pointed out the difficulty of proving an offence was committed while abroad, saying, 'The very fact of going is not an offence'. It is also worth noting that none of the four terror attacks in London and Manchester in 2017 were carried out by returnees from Iraq and Syria, although the Manchester bomber Salman Abedi had fought in Libya.

Case study: radicalisation

In recent years, evidence has emerged that radicalisation of many young, potentially vulnerable, male and female citizens is becoming more commonplace. Although far fewer are traveling to places like Syria since ISIS lost control of much of its territory, there are still major concerns about the use of methods such as social media to radicalise young people. This is seen from the figures released for 2018 by the Prevent Programmes of people referring to the deradicalisation process. From a total of over 7,000 individuals, 57% were under 20 years of age, 87% were male, and 44% were referred for concerns related to Islamist extremism and 18% for right-wing extremism. Of the total number of referrals, over two-thirds came from schools and the police.

Case study: terrorist plots uncovered

Although the number of terrorist arrests in the UK has fallen in recent years, the UK Threat Level has remained at or above Severe since 2014. It has, however been reduced to Substantial as of late-2019 except in Northern Ireland where it remains at Severe. This is an indication of how difficult the prevention of terrorism is. Currently, the UK faces threats from several sources including Islamist and right-wing extremists as well as a growing threat from dissident Irish Republican groups. In September of 2019 there were 800 'live' investigations. The UK's most senior counter-terrorism police officer, Neil Basu stated at that time that 22 terror plots had been foiled since the Westminster attack including seven related to far-right terror.

Across Europe, according to figures released by Europol (Europe's law enforcement agency) for 2017/18 a total of 205 plots had been foiled or failed, which was a 45% increase on the previous year. Although terrorism is still a very rare event in Europe compared with other parts of the world, an expert in terrorism from The Royal Institute of International Affairs stated that, 'It is simply impossible to prevent every single attack, especially those carried out by lone actors with low tech means and little support from other individuals'.

TOP TIP

Mapping terrorism: the following link will give you further information about terrorism worldwide: https://www.mi5.gov.uk/international-terrorism

Quick Test

1. What evidence is there that counter terrorism tactics have been successful in the UK and Europe?
2. Describe the types of individuals referred to the Prevent Programme for deradicalisation.
3. What are the sources of the main threats currently facing the UK?
4. According to the expert from The Royal Institute of International Affairs, which types of attack are most difficult to prevent?

Higher
MODERN STUDIES

For SQA 2019 and beyond

Practice Papers

Donna Ford and Fiona Weir

Introduction

This book is to help you with your preparations for the Higher Modern Studies exam. It contains two practice papers that show the layout of the exam, the question types and an idea of how each of the different types of questions are marked. You may wish to dip into the papers as you study a certain topic but it's probably a good idea to sit a whole paper nearer the exam so you get an idea of the time pressure involved.

Course and question paper structure

Higher Modern Studies is marked out of 110. The question paper is worth 80 marks and the assignment is worth 30 marks. In the question paper there are three sections, one section will be worth 12 marks and the other two will be worth 20 marks. The sections are divided up as follows:

- Democracy in Scotland and the United Kingdom – refer to either or both.

- Social Issues in the United Kingdom – complete questions on **EITHER** Social Inequality **OR** Crime and the Law.

- International Issues – complete questions on a World Power **OR** a World Issue.

Make sure you know which option you have studied

For the third section, you will have studied a G20 country for World Powers such as the USA or China. The questions asked will not refer specifically to the USA or China but will say 'For a world power you have studied'. Alternatively, if you have studied a World Issue such as Terrorism, the question will not specifically mention that but will say 'For a world issue you have studied'.

The first thing you should write down is what World Power or World Issue you have studied **before** you start to answer the question or integrate the name of the world power or issue you have studied into your introduction.

Question Paper 1 structure

Question Paper 1 is an extended response paper worth a total of 52 marks. You will complete 3 questions in 1 hour 45 minutes:

- 2 × 20-mark knowledge questions.

- 1 × 12-mark knowledge question.

Knowledge questions

Knowledge questions are either for 12 marks or for 20 marks.

12-mark questions

For 12-mark questions, 8 marks are given for knowledge and 4 marks for analysis/evaluation. If more than 4 analysis/evaluation marks are available, these can be credited as knowledge and understanding (KU) if required.

Analyse questions – Candidates will identify parts of an issue, the relationship between these parts and their relationships with the whole; draw out and relate implications.

Evaluate questions – Candidates will make a judgement based on criteria; determine the value of something.

20-mark questions

For 20-mark questions, 8 marks are given for knowledge, 4 for analysis/evaluation, 6 for conclusions and 2 for structure.

Discuss questions – Candidates will communicate ideas and information on the issue in the statement. Candidates will be credited for analysing and evaluating different views of the statement/viewpoint.

You must show knowledge, analysis, evaluation and show a clear, coherent structure – think introduction, paragraphs and a final conclusion but also that your points are made in a logical and coherent order.

To what extent questions – Candidates will analyse the issue in the question and come to a conclusion or conclusions that involve an evaluative judgement that is likely to be quantitative in nature.

You must show knowledge, analysis, evaluation and show a clear, coherent structure – think introduction, paragraphs and a final conclusion but also that your points are made in a logical and coherent order.

Question Paper 2 structure

Question Paper 2 is a source-based question paper worth 28 marks. You will complete 3 questions in 1 hour 15 minutes:

- 1 x 10 mark degree of accuracy question.
- 1 x 10 mark conclusions question.
- 1 x 8 mark reliability of sources question.

Skills questions

These will appear in the section where there is not a 20-mark essay. They are worth 8 marks.

To what extent is the view accurate questions

You are asked to identify, using up to **three** sources, where the given view is correct or not. Again, for the full 10 marks, you must make an overall judgement as to whether the view is supported by evidence.

Drawing conclusions questions

You will be asked to draw **three** conclusions on a subject. Depending on the amount of evidence you use from the three sources, you can gain up to 3 marks per conclusion. Try and link evidence from different sources or indeed within different parts of the same source. In order to gain full marks you will need to come to an overall conclusion on the issue **AND** use all the sources. No marks are awarded for just the conclusions without any evidence.

Reliability of sources question

You will be asked to comment on the reliability of three different sources. The sources may be written, graphical, numerical or pictorial. You have also to come to a decision regarding which of the three sources is the **most reliable**.

Handy hints

Be organised

Boring as it may be, organisation is the key to success. Make sure your folder is organised – put all your notes and information into the right unit section. Make sure that you look at essays and skills questions that you have done and understand the feedback your teacher has given you. If you don't, go back and ask them.

Remember it's **Modern** Studies – your World Issues, all evidence and examples quoted should come from the last 10 years at the very latest.

In question paper 1 you have two 20-mark essay questions to do, and one 12-mark question to complete. It is a good idea to do the 20-mark questions first so you don't run out of time. Spend roughly about 45 minutes on these questions and 25 minutes on the 12-mark response. Many candidates can describe and explain knowledge very well in the questions but there is a lack of discussion and analysis – see above.

In question paper 2 you have two 10-mark skills-based questions to do and one 8-mark question. Aim to spend roughly 30 minutes on each of the 10-mark questions and the remaining 15 minutes on the 8-mark question.

Be specific

Candidates can lose out on marks because they just make very general statements without explaining more or quoting evidence to back things up; for example, 'poor people don't live as long'. This statement is very vague, is not well explained and has no statistics or evidence to back it up.

Refer to the question – make sure you answer it. If the question asks you 'To what extent does the media influence people to vote a certain way?' you must keep referring back to that – how much of an influence was that type of media in influencing the way that people vote?

It's good practice to write the question at the top of the question paper so you can see it as you write your essay.

The assignment

This is worth 30 marks (one-third of the total marks) and is externally assessed. This means it is sent to the SQA to be marked. You will work on it throughout the year and it has to be written up under exam conditions. You will get 1 hour 30 mins to do this at a time decided by your teacher.

Structure and layout are important – the assignment must be in the form of a report and is not a continuous essay. There's no one correct style to follow but the report must include all the information that you have decided to include. A suggested structure would be as follows:

- Introduction – to include a detailed background to your issue (see below)
- The options you have to decide between
- Role and remit
- Recommendation
- Arguments for recommendation
- Consideration of opposing arguments and rebuttal
- Conclusion
- Evaluation of sources

Mark allocation

1. Identifying and demonstrating knowledge and understanding of the issue about which a decision is to be made, including alternative courses of action. Candidates can be credited in a number of ways up to a maximum of 10 marks.

2. Analysing and synthesising information from a range of sources including use of specified resources. Candidates can be credited in a number of ways up to a maximum of 10 marks.

3. Evaluating the usefulness and reliability of a range of sources of information. Candidates can be credited in a number of ways up to a maximum of 2 marks.

4. Communicating information using the conventions of a report. Candidates can be credited in a number of ways up to a maximum of 4 marks.

5. Reaching a decision, supported by evidence, about the issue. Candidates can be credited in a number of ways up to a maximum of 4 marks.

Make sure you state your recommendation at the start of the report – this keeps you focused on what you are arguing for.

The resource sheet is two sides of A4 that show evidence of your research, which you can take in to the write-up. It is not a plan and if you set it out as such, you may lose marks from your structure allocation. You should refer to and use all the sources on the resource sheet but don't use sources that are not on the sheet. No marks will be given for straight copying from the source sheet.

You must source where your information has come from on your resource sheet. If using newspapers, state the publisher, date and headline. If using a website, make sure you give the publisher and date that the website was accessed on the resource sheet.

Pupils should use more technical language – Higher pupils should be able to do this, e.g. instead of 'poor areas', use 'areas of deprivation'.

Ten marks are allocated for knowledge. It is good practice to start with a detailed introduction that explains the issue fully and sets the background scene, politically, socially and perhaps internationally. This will enable you to pick up some good knowledge marks straight away.

You can refer to the same source more than once for different arguments and get credit for each reference.

Marks are given for evaluating your sources so be specific when you are evaluating them. Use words such as reliable, useful, bias, accurate and up-to-date.

Quick Guide to the Exam Paper

QUESTION PAPER 1	
Section 1: Democracy in Scotland and the United Kingdom	Choice of **three** questions in the paper
Section 2: Social issues in the United Kingdom Option 1: Social Inequality **OR** Option 2: Crime and the Law	Choice of **two** questions in each option
Section 3: International Issues Option 1: World Powers **OR** Option 2: International Issues	Choice of **two** questions in each option

NOTE: You must complete only **ONE** question from each section of the question paper. Remember that the 20-mark questions can appear across all sections of the paper as can the 12-mark question.

QUESTION PAPER 2
Question 1: Drawing conclusions question
Question 2: To what extent is the view accurate question
Question 3: Reliability of sources question
NOTE: You must attempt **ALL** of the questions in the question paper.

Practice Paper A

Higher Modern Studies

Practice Papers for SQA Exams

Practice Paper A
Paper 1

Duration — 1 hour 45 minutes

Total marks — 52

SECTION 1 — DEMOCRACY IN SCOTLAND AND THE UNITED KINGDOM — 20 marks

Attempt **ONE** question from 1(a) **OR** 1(b) **OR** 1(c)

SECTION 2 — SOCIAL ISSUES IN THE UNITED KINGDOM — 12 marks

       Part A Social inequality

       Part B Crime and the law

Attempt **ONE** question from 2(a) **OR** 2(b) **OR** 2(c) **OR** 2(d)

SECTION 3 — INTERNATIONAL ISSUES — 20 marks

       Part C World powers

       Part D World issues

Attempt **ONE** question from 3(a) **OR** 3(b) **OR** 3(c) **OR** 3(d)

Write your answers clearly in the answer booklet provided. In the answer booklet, you must clearly identify the question number you are attempting.

Use **blue** or **black** ink.

Before leaving the examination room you must give your answer booklet to the Invigilator; if you do not, you may lose all the marks for this paper.

Exam A — Paper 1

SECTION 1 — DEMOCRACY IN SCOTLAND AND THE UNITED KINGDOM — 20 marks

Attempt **EITHER** Question 1(a) **OR** 1(b) **OR** 1(c)

Question 1

(a) | *Social class is still the most important factor in determining voting behaviour.* |

Discuss.

You should refer to Scotland **or** the United Kingdom **or** both in your answer.

20

OR

(b) | *The electoral systems used to elect representatives in the United Kingdom have many strengths and weaknesses.* |

Discuss.

You should refer to Scotland **or** the United Kingdom **or** both in your answer.

20

OR

(c) | *There are a number of alternative ways of governing Scotland.* |

Discuss.

You should refer to Scotland **or** the United Kingdom **or** both in your answer.

20

SECTION 2 — SOCIAL ISSUES IN THE UNITED KINGDOM — 12 marks

Attempt QUESTION 2(a) OR 2(b) OR 2(c) OR 2(d)

Question 2

Part A: Social inequality

Answers may refer to Scotland **or** the United Kingdom **or** both.

(a)   Analyse the reasons why health inequalities exist.   **12**

OR

(b)   Evaluate the effectiveness of measures taken to tackle inequality.   **12**

OR

Part B: Crime and the law

Answers may refer to Scotland **or** the United Kingdom **or** both.

(c)   Analyse the different theories of the causes of crime.   **12**

OR

(d)   Evaluate the effectiveness of custodial responses to crime.   **12**

EXAM PAPER A — SECTION 3 — INTERNATIONAL ISSUES — 20 marks

Attempt **ONE** Question **FROM** 3(a) **OR** 3(b) **OR** 3(c) **OR** 3(d)

Question 3

Part C: World powers

With reference to a world power you have studied:

(a) To what extent does the political system allow political participation by all citizens? **20**

OR

(b) To what extent have government responses to socio-economic inequality been effective? **20**

OR

Part D: World issues

With reference to a world issue you have studied:

(c) To what extent does the issue have an effect on individuals and their families? **20**

OR

(d) To what extent has the response by international organisations been effective? **20**

[END OF PRACTICE QUESTION PAPER]

Higher Modern Studies

Practice Papers for SQA Exams

Practice Paper A
Paper 2

Duration — 1 hour 15 minutes

Total marks — 28

Attempt **ALL** questions

Write your answers clearly in the answer booklet provided. In the answer booklet, you must clearly identify the question number you are attempting.

Use **blue** or **black** ink.

Before leaving the examination room you must give your answer booklet to the Invigilator; if you do not, you may lose all the marks for this paper.

×Leckie
the education publisher
for Scotland

Total marks — 28

Attempt **ALL** questions

Question 1

Study Sources A, B and C then attempt the question that follows.

SOURCE A

The Knife Crime Crisis Sweeping England & Wales

According to recent reports, the levels of recorded knife crime in England & Wales have increased for the fifth consecutive year in a row. The Office for National Statistics (ONS) confirmed that 40,577 offences were recorded in 2018, which is a sizeable increase since 2011. In contrast, that level of knife crime in Scotland has fallen since the Scottish Government introduced it multi-agency approach to tackle the problem that saw a United Nations report label it the most violent country in the developed world.

London has been the worst affected region of England & Wales and has seen a rapid increase in the number of crimes involving knifes. In the first six months of 2019 there have been 86 knife crime deaths in London many of which have been widely reported in the media as acts of cowardly violence against innocent by standers such as the Zahir Visiter, 25, who was stabbed to death for a £60,000 watch he was wearing.

What is also clear is that dealing with this deteriorating situation has become a political football as politicians and the government scrabble to deal with it. Even President Donald Trump has made his views known, criticising the Mayor of London, Sadiq Khan's inaction, who in turn has blamed the UK Government police budget cuts. The growing problem has seen many young males become so fearful of becoming a victim of knife crime that they start carrying and consequently using knifes as a means of protection.

Authorities in England & Wales have drawn heavy criticism is in their handling of the crisis. One region in particular, Nottinghamshire, has been ridiculed for distributing domestic violence victims with blunt knifes in an attempt to protect them. Other solutions, such as keeping schools open at weekends and extending school hours have been criticised by interests groups as not tackling the root cause of the problem, which according to Mothers Against Violence is the fact than many young males brought up in unstable and chaotic home environments normalise the carrying and use of sharp instruments. Likewise, the proposal by a Conservative MP, Scott Mann, to fit GPS trackers to all knifes sold was seen as laughable by the public and the British media.

(continued)

Commentators have, however, pointed to the success of the Scottish Government Model in reducing violent crime to a 40-year low. The multi-agency approach led by Police Scotland and the creation of the Violence Reduction Unit (VRU) has helped rescue many young Scottish males from the revolving door of prison and provided them with the skills and qualifications they need to turn their life around. The highly successful 'Street and Arrow' café programme has proved highly successful in allowing offenders to get a foot on the employment ladder. Most notably, Callum Hutchinson, who was stabbed nine times in front of his young son, before being saved by the VRU's Navigator Programme based in Glasgow's Royal Infirmary. So successful was Callum's rehabilitation, that he now tours the country, working with the VRU, as a guest speaker. Furthermore, the work of the VRU and charities like, 'Medics Against Violence', has meant that young people across Scotland are now far less likely to carry a knife having been educated on the horrific consequences of doing so.

SOURCE B

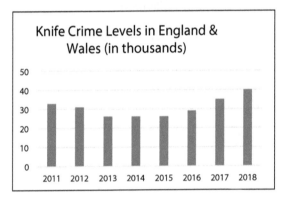

Knife Crime Levels in England & Wales (in thousands)

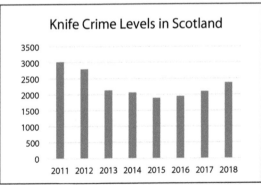

Knife Crime Levels in Scotland

SOURCE C

Gender & age of victims stabbed to death

Number of people killed in England and Wales in 2017-18 by age
Female   Male

Gender & age of knife crime suspects

Number of suspects in English and Wales in 2017-18 by age group
Female   Male

Attempt the following question, using only the information in Sources A, B and C.

What conclusions can be drawn about the knife crime in England and Wales?

You must draw conclusions about:

- the overall trend in knife crime levels in England and Wales compared to Scotland

- the group most likely to be affected by knife crime in England and Wales

- the success of the government strategies to deal with knife crime

You must give an overall conclusion about the **extent** of knife crime in England and Wales.

10

Question 2

Study Sources A, B and C then attempt the question that follows.

SOURCE A

Voters tired of FPTP and Demand Change

There is a growing tide of support in the United Kingdom to review our current legislative arrangements. According to a recent poll commissioned by the *Independent* newspaper voters are unhappy with the use of First-Past-the-Post (FPTP) used to elect MPs to the House of Commons. The poll concluded that only 4% of voters feel properly represented at Westminster. This echoes the views of the popular campaign group, Electoral Reform Society (ERS) who claim in their new publication, 'Westminster Beyond Brexit' that many citizens feel disenfranchised by the undemocratic nature of the current system.

This change of opinion is a major U-turn since the 2011 AV Referendum results clearly showed that the electorate did not want to see FPTP replaced. The overwhelming majority of voters supported the continued use of FPTP while just 32% of voters supported the use of AV to elect MPs to the House of Commons.

Many critics argue that the disproportionate results produced by FPTP are clearly undemocratic and demonstrate the unfairness of the system. For example, in 2015 the SNP gained 95% of the available Scottish seats when only half of the Scottish electorate voted for them. Moreover, the 2019 Peterborough by-election saw Labour return the winning candidate with only 30% of the votes cast. Most recently, the electorate have raised concerns following the resignation of Theresa May as Prime Minister when Boris Johnson was elected as leader of the Conservative Party and subsequently became Prime Minister after the 160,000 Conservative membership voted for their party leader.

Supporters of the FPTP system argue that there is no need to change the current system as it returns a strong stable government to office who can then carry out its manifesto promises without having to rely on backroom deals and compromises with smaller parties. In addition, we should not reform the current system as FPTP has ensured that the rise of extremist parties, like the BNP, do not gain power in Westminster.

SOURCE B

Readers – have your say!

'The whole political system needs to be brought into the 21st century. Westminster is being run for the sake of a rich political elite and it's time for the working-class people of Britain to get their country back.' **N.Pott, Chichester**

'Our voting system isn't just unfair – it's tearing the country apart – creating division and disunity amongst voters.' **E. Winters, Member of the ERS, Glasgow**

'The biggest afront to democracy is that 0.2% of the electorate decided that Boris Johnson should be our next Prime Minister simply because they paid their £25 membership to the Conservative Party.' **L. Campbell, Newcastle**

'The Lords are unelected and accountable to no-one. Once appointed they are free to claim expenses and allowances for next to nothing. They clearly do not provide value for money for the taxpayer and the public support further reform.' **R. Kellechan, Motherwell**

'The Lords is a busy and effective chamber and in 2018 made more than 200 changes to legislation and produced over 200 Committee reports. They certainly offer value for money and need no further modernisation.' **G. Craig, former civil servant, Kensington**

SOURCE C

The House of Lords – Out of Date?

A recent YouGov poll has concluded that the voting public are 'largely apathetic' about the Upper Chamber of the UK Parliament. This reiterates the findings of previous polling that has shown the UK public do not believe that previous reforms to the House of Lords have gone far enough. Currently, the House of Lords acts as a check on the House of Commons and can revise and delay laws. Lords – called peers – are currently all appointed by the government apart from a minority that continue to hold hereditary titles.

Recent reports have questioned the value for money offered by the Lords. The Electoral Reform Society has brought to light the 'scandal of the silent peers'. An ERS research report concluded that 115 Lords failed to speak in the chamber despite claiming their £305 per day expenses. One Peer, Lord Irvine of Lairg, only spoke once in twelve months but claimed £40,050 in expenses. Similarly, Baroness Mone has only spoken four times in the chamber since her appointment in 2015.

However, there are those who argue the Lords performs an important role within our democracy. There is no doubt that the Lords has used their powers to scrutinise the work of the government and effect change. The Health and Social Care 2012 Bill was not given an easy passage by the Lords when it navigated the Commons relatively smoothly. Likewise, the Lords revolt against the Tax Credit changes that the government wished to introduce also proves that they hold the Government of the day to account.

Supporters of the Lords also argue that it has become more democratic in recent years as the social diversity of the House of Lords has improved. Women now account for 204 Peers – 26%, while 51 Peers come from a black or minority background – 6%. Even so, the average age of the 800 Peers is 69 years of age with the majority of the Peers being university graduates and 57% of Peers privately educated.

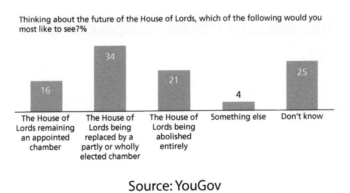

Thinking about the future of the House of Lords, which of the following would you most like to see?%

The House of Lords remaining an appointed chamber	The House of Lords being replaced by a partly or wholly elected chamber	The House of Lords being abolished entirely	Something else	Don't know
16	34	21	4	25

Source: YouGov

Attempt the following question, using only the information in Sources A, B and C.

To what extent is it accurate to state that there is a clear desire to modernise the UK Parliament.

10

Question 3

Study Sources A, B and C then attempt the question that follows.

SOURCE A

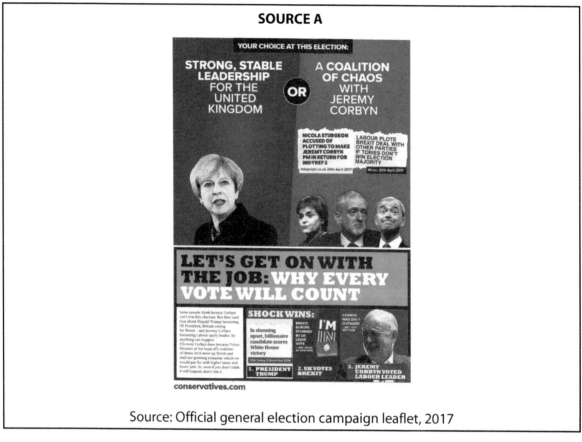

Source: Official general election campaign leaflet, 2017

SOURCE B

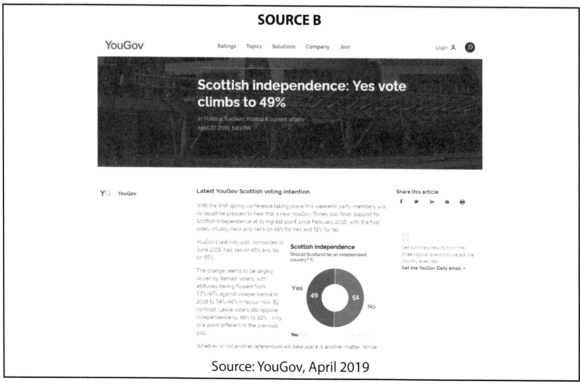

Source: YouGov, April 2019

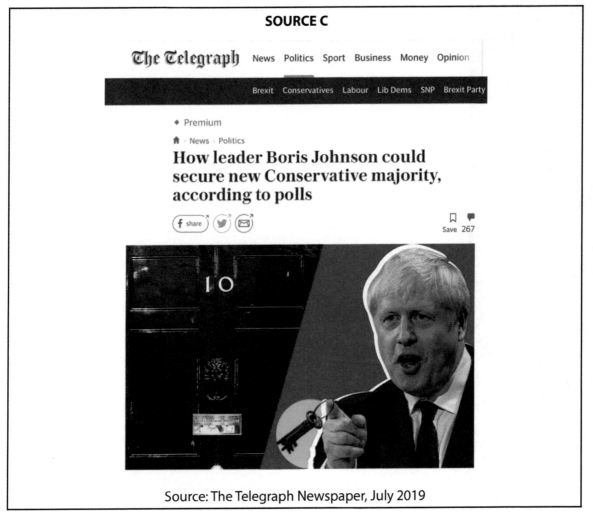

Source: The Telegraph Newspaper, July 2019

Attempt the following question, using only the information in Sources A, B and C.

To what extent are Sources A, B and C reliable?

You must provide an overall conclusion on the most reliable source of information.   **8**

[END OF PRACTICE QUESTION PAPER]

Practice Paper B

Higher Modern Studies

Practice Papers for SQA Exams

Practice Paper B
Paper 1

Duration — 1 hour 45 minutes

Total marks — 52

SECTION 1 — DEMOCRACY IN SCOTLAND AND THE UNITED KINGDOM — 12 marks

Answer **ONE** question from 1(a) **OR** 1(b) **OR** 1(c)

SECTION 2 — SOCIAL ISSUES IN THE UNITED KINGDOM — 20 marks

      Part A Social inequality

      Part B Crime and the law

Attempt **ONE** question from 2(a) **OR** 2(b) **OR** 2(c) **OR** 2(d)

SECTION 3 — INTERNATIONAL ISSUES — 20 marks

      Part C World powers

      Part D World issues

Attempt **ONE** question from 3(a) **OR** 3(b) **OR** 3(c) **OR** 3(d)

Write your answers clearly in the answer booklet provided. In the answer booklet, you must clearly identify the question number you are attempting.

Use **blue** or **black** ink.

Before leaving the examination room you must give your answer booklet to the Invigilator; if you do not, you may lose all the marks for this paper.

×Leckie
the education publisher
for Scotland

Exam B — Paper 1

SECTION 1 — DEMOCRACY IN SCOTLAND AND THE UNITED KINGDOM — 12 marks

Attempt **EITHER** Question 1(a) **OR** 1(b) **OR** 1(c)

Question 1

(a)   Evaluate whether media is a major factor in influencing voting behaviour.

You should refer to Scotland **or** the United Kingdom **or** both in your answer.   **12**

OR

(b)   Evaluate whether all citizens are able to influence government decision making.

You should refer to Scotland **or** the United Kingdom **or** both in your answer.   **12**

OR

(c)   Evaluate the implications of the United Kingdom leaving the EU.

You should refer to Scotland **or** the United Kingdom **or** both in your answer.   **12**

SECTION 2 — SOCIAL ISSUES IN THE UNITED KINGDOM — 20 marks

Attempt Question 2(a) **OR** 2(b) **OR** 2(c) **OR** 2(d)

Question 2

Part A: Social inequality

Answers may refer to Scotland **or** the United Kingdom **or** both.

(a)   To what extent does inequality affect a group (or groups) in society today?   **20**

OR

(b)   *The government has the main responsibility in tackling inequality.* Discuss.   **20**

OR

Part B: Crime and the law

Answers may refer to Scotland **or** the United Kingdom **or** both.

(c)   *Crime has a major social and economic impact on society.* Discuss.   **20**

OR

(d)   To what extent are non-custodial sentences effective in tackling crime?   **20**

EXAM PAPER B — SECTION 3 — INTERNATIONAL ISSUES — 20 marks

Attempt **ONE** question from 3(a) **OR** 3(b) **OR** 3(c) **OR** 3(d)

Question 3

Part C: World powers

With reference to a world power you have studied:

(a)   To what extent does it have an influence on the rest of the world?   **20**

OR

(b) | *Socio-economic inequality has a major impact on groups in society.* | Discuss.   **20**

OR

Part D: World issues

With reference to a world issue you have studied:

(c) | *There are many social and economic factors which have caused the issue.* | Discuss.   **20**

OR

(d)   To what extent has it had an impact on the governments involved and the wider international community?   **20**

[END OF PRACTICE QUESTION PAPER]

Higher Modern Studies

Practice Papers for SQA Exams

Practice Paper B
Paper 2

Duration — 1 hour 15 minutes

Total marks — 28

Attempt **ALL** questions

Write your answers clearly in the answer booklet provided. In the answer booklet, you must clearly identify the question number you are attempting.

Use **blue** or **black** ink.

Before leaving the examination room you must give your answer booklet to the Invigilator; if you do not, you may lose all the marks for this paper.

Total marks — 28

Attempt **ALL** questions

Question 1

Study Sources A, B and C then attempt the question that follows.

SOURCE A

2017 General Election – A new dawn in campaigning?

Following the success of the 2015 leaders debates, the 2017 debates proved a bit of a damp squib. The enthusiasm for the debates had dwindled not only in the eyes of the viewing public but also in the eyes of the party leaders when both Theresa May and Jeremey Corbyn decided that they would not take part in the live debates. The political editor of ITV, Robert Peston, even labelled the decision by both leaders not to participate as 'pathetic'. In Theresa May's absence her political opponents took the opportunity to criticise her decision. Caroline Lucas of the Green Party argued 'that the first rule of leadership is to show up'.

It was also the case that top pollsters for YouGov suggested that 'he saw nothing in the debate(s) that would have a major impact on public opinion.' This was undoubtedly the case with one-third of viewers switching off less than halfway through the two-hour slot. The sad fact of the matter is that more people choose to watch an episode of 'Supervet' than the first leaders' debate.

Many commentators suggested that the lack of interest in the election campaign overall was down to the projected results reported in the media by polling organisations such as Mori, ICM, Survation and YouGov who implied the election result was all but a forgone conclusion with the Conservative party securing a significantly larger share of the vote compared to Labour. For the six weeks of campaigning, the polls consistently gave the incumbent government a significant lead in the polls ranging from 21% (YouGov) at the start of the campaign to an 11% (ICM) lead at the beginning of June.

It was also evident that traditional campaigning methods were being challenged by social media as an electoral influence. The political journal, *The Spectator,* ran a story arguing that 'Politics [was] now a digital arms race, and Labour is Winning.' The Labour Party's use of social media platforms such as Twitter, Facebook and online videos to engage younger voters (18–24yrs) is thought to explain why Labour's percentage share of the vote increased by nearly ten percent on their 2015 performance.

Despite the lack of enthusiasm for the live TV debates during the campaign, a study by YouGov later concluded that the public believed that 'traditional media mattered more in the 2017 general election'. They argued that while the increased use of social media helped to stimulate the interest of younger voters, as a whole the voting public still considered the 'old media' more influential when deciding who to vote for.

SOURCE B

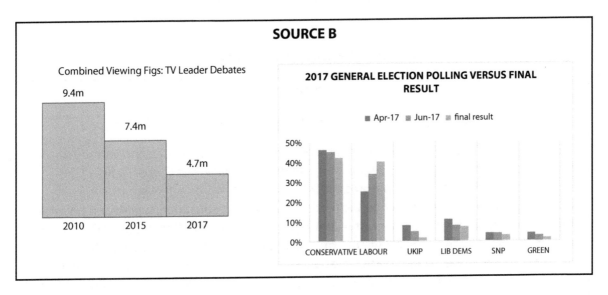

Combined Viewing Figs: TV Leader Debates

9.4m — 2010
7.4m — 2015
4.7m — 2017

2017 GENERAL ELECTION POLLING VERSUS FINAL RESULT

■ Apr-17 ■ Jun-17 ■ final result

CONSERVATIVE LABOUR UKIP LIB DEMS SNP GREEN

SOURCE C

	Twitter Followers	Facebook Followers
Theresa May (Conservative)	411,000	540,000
Jeremy Corbyn (Labour)	1,600,000	1,400,000

And how much influence, if any, do you think each of the following had in helping you choose who to vote for or in confirming your choice of who to vote for?%

■ All GB ■ 18-24

	All GB	18-24
Television	42	54
Family members	32	32
Newspapers, magazines	32	28
Friends and colleagues	32	48
Social media	26	50
Radio	25	25

Attempt the following question, using only the information in Sources A, B and C.

What conclusions can be drawn about the 2017 General Election?

You must draw conclusions about:

- The accuracy of polling projections made compared to the actual results.

- The public interest in the TV leaders' debate compared to previous elections.

- The importance of social media in the 2017 General Election Campaign.

You must give an overall conclusion about the most influential form of the media during the campaign.

10

Question 2

Study Sources A, B and C then attempt the question that follows.

SOURCE A

Inequality between Men and Women in the European Union

A key aim of the European Union is to bring about equality between men and women in all aspects of life including health, education and the workplace. The Global Gender Gap Report annually documents the progress of 149 countries towards achieving true equality within their society in areas of economic participation(work), education, health and political empowerment. According to the most recent report, some EU countries are amongst the most equal in the world with Germany 14th out of 149. Some of the newer countries do less well, with the Czech Republic in 82nd place, Croatia 59th and Estonia at 33rd place. While there has been considerable progress made over the years, more has to be done as inequalities still exist in newer member states.

Although women usually live longer than men, the EU is concerned with men's health as much as that of women. Average life expectancy and quality of life for men and women have increased over the last sixty years but there are still differences between countries. Certain diseases affect men more than women and vice versa. Smoking is more common among men than women in all EU countries and this has an impact on diseases such as strokes, cancer and heart disease.

There has been an increase in unemployment across the EU and this has affected men more than women in some countries. When it comes to pay, women still earn less than men in every single member state of the EU although the gender pay gap is narrower in some countries compared to others. Many women are employed in part-time work and this tends to bring the average wage down. This means women experience higher levels of poverty and social exclusion than men. In professional occupations, women are making some progress but still lag behind men especially at boardroom level.

In education, within the EU, females tend to outnumber males at college or university and in the future, this may result in the gender pay gap decreasing and more women ending up in better-paid jobs. In all EU states, literacy levels are very similar for males and females.

In terms of political representation, women have made some progress gaining entry to the high levels of political office although the political gender gap stubbornly remains the biggest area of inequality. In terms of representation, the average tenure of women as head of state or prime minister is a pitiful 2 years. However, women have done much better securing positions as cabinet members and government ministers.

SOURCE B

Information on Education, Political Office and Employment in Selected EU Countries

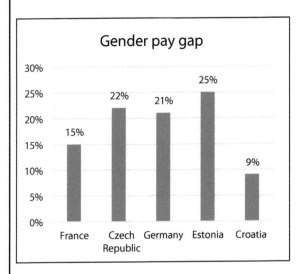

Gender pay gap

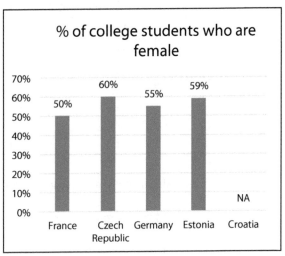

% of college students who are female

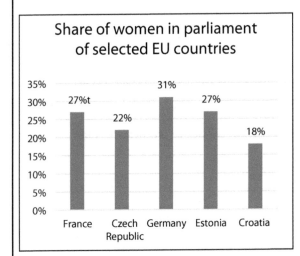

Share of women in parliament of selected EU countries

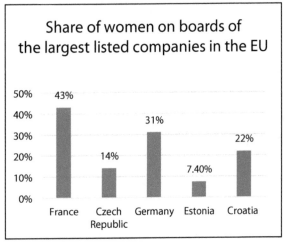

Share of women on boards of the largest listed companies in the EU

SOURCE C

Deaths per 100,000 resulting from diseases linked to smoking						
	Lung cancer		Heart disease		Stroke	
	Male	Female	Male	Female	Male	Female
France	48	15	77	32	53	42
Czech Republic	53	16	388	253	124	104
Germany	42	16	189	101	65	59
Estonia	51	9	388	211	93	66
Croatia	56	14	341	244	210	173

Information on health and life expectancy from selected EU countries by sex

Life expectancy by sex		
	Male	Female
France	79.2	85.5
Czech Republic	75.7	81.6
Germany	78.3	83.1
Estonia	73.2	82.2
Croatia	74.4	80.5

Attempt the following question, using only the information in Sources A, B and C.

To what extent is it accurate to state that the EU has been successful in eradicating inequalities in all areas?

10

Question 3

Study Sources A and B, then attempt the question that follows.

SOURCE A

School of Education

Who's in prison? A snapshot of Scotland's prison population

How many people are in prison in Scotland?

Figures for July 2015 showed there were **8,062 prisoners** held in prisons across Scotland. Due to releases and court outcomes, exact numbers change from day to day, and even within each day. At any given time, around 300 prisoners are on Home Detention Curfew (HDC), which means they are living at home adhering to a curfew and wearing an electronic monitor.

Scotland has 15 prisons. 13 prisons are public and are run by the Scottish Prison Service (SPS), and two are privately run for profit under contract to the SPS. The majority of prisons are located across the Central Belt of Scotland (this is also the most densely populated section of the country), though there are prisons across the country. If you want to more about this, the Scottish Prison Service (SPS) website has detailed information about each prison.

SOURCE B

'Emergency' warning as number of prison assaults rises

By STV News
🕘 9 Jun 2019 9:38 am

An MSP has claimed that Scotland's jails are in a "state of emergency".

An MSP has claimed that Scotland's jails are in a "state of emergency" as figures indicate that the total number of prison assaults are at a five-year high.

Following a Freedom of Information request by the Scottish Liberal Democrats, figures indicate that there has been a rise in the number of assaults on prisoners by other prisoners, as well as assaults on staff by prisoners.

The total number of serious prisoner on prisoner assaults in Scottish prisons increased from 94 in 2017/18 to 135 in 2018/19, whilst assaults which caused either minor or no injuries rose from 2,120 to 2,995 over the same period.

In 2014/15, there was a total of 66 serious prisoner on prisoner assaults, and 1,778 assaults with minor or no injuries caused.

The largest increase in the number of serious assaults was recorded at HMP Kilmarnock, which saw prisoner on prisoner serious assaults rise by 14 from 2 in 2017/18 to 16 in the latest statistics.

HMP Perth saw the most significant decrease in this category over the same period, with a fall by 7 from 15 serious prisoner on prisoner assaults to 8 in 2018/2019.

The highest number of prisoner on prisoner assaults with either minor or no injuries caused was recorded at HMP Polmont – the number rose to 606 in 2018/19, an increase on the 518 for the previous year.

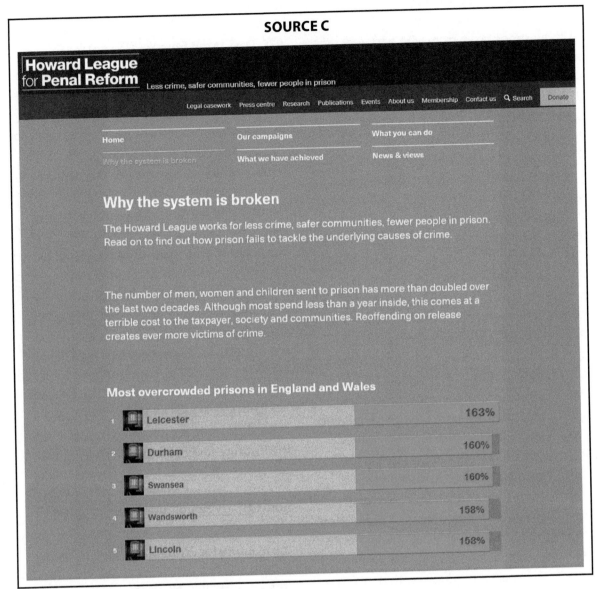

SOURCE C

Attempt the following question, using only the information in Sources A, B and C.

To what extent are Sources A, B and C reliable?

You must provide an overall conclusion on the most reliable source of information.

8

[END OF QUESTION PAPER]

Text permissions

P12: Questions taken from SQA past and specimen papers reproduced with permission, copyright © Scottish Qualifications Authority.

P15: Questions taken from SQA past and specimen papers reproduced with permission, copyright © Scottish Qualifications Authority.

P16: Questions taken from SQA past and specimen papers reproduced with permission, copyright © Scottish Qualifications Authority.

P17: Questions taken from SQA past and specimen papers reproduced with permission, copyright © Scottish Qualifications Authority.

P18: Questions taken from SQA past and specimen papers reproduced with permission, copyright © Scottish Qualifications Authority.

P19: Questions taken from SQA past and specimen papers reproduced with permission, copyright © Scottish Qualifications Authority.

P20: Questions taken from SQA past and specimen papers reproduced with permission, copyright © Scottish Qualifications Authority.

P21: Data reproduced with permission from Social Research Institute, Ipsos MORI.

P21: Questions taken from SQA past and specimen papers reproduced with permission, copyright © Scottish Qualifications Authority.

P22: Questions taken from SQA past and specimen papers reproduced with permission, copyright © Scottish Qualifications Authority.

P40: Quotation taken from the Scottish Independence Referendum Act 2013.

P40: Quotation by David Cameron.

P40: Quotation by Alex Salmond, taken from *The Andrew Marr Show*.

P57: Data reproduced with permission from the Electoral Reform Society.

P66: Data reproduced with permission from the Social Research Institute, Ipsos MORI

P67: Quotation reproduced with permission from the Social Research Institute, Ipsos MORI.

P70: Data taken from YouGov.co.uk.

P72: Data reproduced with permission from the British Election Study.

P79: Data taken from YouGov.co.uk.

P92: Quotation by Peter Townsend, taken from the Child Poverty Action Group.

P151: Quotation reproduced with permission from The National Alliance to End Homelessness. www.endhomelessness.org

P167: Quotation used with permission from the Institute for Economics & Peace: Global Terrorism Index 2018: Measuring the Impact of Terrorism, Sydney, November 2018. Available from http://visionofhumanity.org/reports.

P168: Quotation used with permission from the Institute for Economics & Peace: Global Terrorism Index 2018: Measuring the Impact of Terrorism, Sydney, November 2018. Available from http://visionofhumanity.org/reports

P168: Data reproduced with permission from the Institute for Economics & Peace: Global Terrorism Index 2018: Measuring the Impact of Terrorism, Sydney, November 2018. Available from http://visionofhumanity.org/reports

P169; Data reproduced with permission from the Institute for Economics & Peace: Global Terrorism Index 2018: Measuring the Impact of Terrorism, Sydney, November 2018. Available from http://visionofhumanity.org/reports

P174: Quotation used with permission from the Institute for Economics & Peace: Global Terrorism Index 2014: Measuring the Impact of Terrorism, Sydney, November 2014. Available from http://visionofhumanity.org/reports

P176: Quotation used with permission from the Institute for Economics & Peace: Global Terrorism Index 2018: Measuring the Impact of Terrorism, Sydney, November 2018. Available from http://visionofhumanity.org/reports

P216: Quotation taken from *The Spectator*.